T	W	T	F	S	S	M	T	W	T	F	S	S	M	T	W	T	F	S	S
12	13	14	15	16	17	18	19	20	21	22	23	24	25	26	27	28	29	30	31
16	17	18	19	20	21	22	23	24	25	26	27	28							
16	17	18	19	20	21	22	23	24	25	26	27	28	29	30	31				
13	14	15	16	17	18	19	20	21	22	23	24	25	26	27	28	29	30		
18	19	20	21	22	23	24	25	26	27	28	29	30	31						
15	16	17	18	19	20	21	22	23	24	25	26	27	28	29					
13	14	15	16	17	18	19	20	21	22	23	24	25	26	27	28	29	30	31	
17	18	19	20	21	22	23	24	25	26	27	28	29	30	31					
14	15	16	17	18	19	20	21	22	23	24	25	26	27	28	29	30			
12	13	14	15	16	17	18	19	20	21	22	23	24	25	26	27	28	29	30	31
16	17	18	19	20	21	22	23	24	25	26	27	28	29	30					
14	15	16	17	18	19	20	21	22	23	24	25	26	27	28	29	30	31		

Published by: J.H. Haynes & Co. Ltd.,
Sparkford, Yeovil, Somerset BA22 7JJ, UK
Telephone: 01963 440635
International Telephone: +44 1963 440635
Website: www.haynes.com

Haynes North America Inc.,
859 Lawrence Drive, Newbury Park, California 91320, USA

*Whilst every effort has been made to ensure the accuracy of the information
contained within this diary, J H Haynes & Co. Ltd. cannot be held
responsible for any errors or omissions.*

Haynes Desk Diary **2021**

Personal Details

Name	
Address	
Postcode	
Telephone (Home)	
Telephone (Office)	
Mobile	
Emergency Contact	
E-mail	
National Insurance Number	
Passport Number	

Key Contact Numbers

Name	Name
Phone	Phone
E-mail	E-mail
Name	Name
Phone	Phone
E-mail	E-mail
Name	Name
Phone	Phone
E-mail	E-mail
Name	Name
Phone	Phone
E-mail	E-mail
Name	Name
Phone	Phone
E-mail	E-mail
Name	Name
Phone	Phone
E-mail	E-mail
Name	Name
Phone	Phone
E-mail	E-mail
Name	Name
Phone	Phone
E-mail	E-mail
Name	Name
Phone	Phone
E-mail	E-mail
Name	Name
Phone	Phone
E-mail	E-mail

2020

January
M	T	W	T	F	**S**	**S**
		1	2	3	**4**	**5**
6	7	8	9	10	**11**	**12**
13	14	15	16	17	**18**	**19**
20	21	22	23	24	**25**	**26**
27	28	29	30	31		

February
M	T	W	T	F	**S**	**S**
					1	**2**
3	4	5	6	7	**8**	**9**
10	11	12	13	14	**15**	**16**
17	18	19	20	21	**22**	**23**
24	25	26	27	28	**29**	

March
M	T	W	T	F	**S**	**S**
						1
2	3	4	5	6	**7**	**8**
9	10	11	12	13	**14**	**15**
16	17	18	19	20	**21**	**22**
23	24	25	26	27	**28**	**29**
30	31					

April
M	T	W	T	F	**S**	**S**
		1	2	3	**4**	**5**
6	7	8	9	10	**11**	**12**
13	14	15	16	17	**18**	**19**
20	21	22	23	24	**25**	**26**
27	28	29	30			

May
M	T	W	T	F	**S**	**S**
				1	**2**	**3**
4	5	6	7	8	**9**	**10**
11	12	13	14	15	**16**	**17**
18	19	20	21	22	**23**	**24**
25	26	27	28	29	**30**	**31**

June
M	T	W	T	F	**S**	**S**
1	2	3	4	5	**6**	**7**
8	9	10	11	12	**13**	**14**
15	16	17	18	19	**20**	**21**
22	23	24	25	26	**27**	**28**
29	30					

July
M	T	W	T	F	**S**	**S**
		1	2	3	**4**	**5**
6	7	8	9	10	**11**	**12**
13	14	15	16	17	**18**	**19**
20	21	22	23	24	**25**	**26**
27	28	29	30	31		

August
M	T	W	T	F	**S**	**S**
					1	**2**
3	4	5	6	7	**8**	**9**
10	11	12	13	14	**15**	**16**
17	18	19	20	21	**22**	**23**
24	25	26	27	28	**29**	**30**
31						

September
M	T	W	T	F	**S**	**S**
	1	2	3	4	**5**	**6**
7	8	9	10	11	**12**	**13**
14	15	16	17	18	**19**	**20**
21	22	23	24	25	**26**	**27**
28	29	30				

October
M	T	W	T	F	**S**	**S**
			1	2	**3**	**4**
5	6	7	8	9	**10**	**11**
12	13	14	15	16	**17**	**18**
19	20	21	22	23	**24**	**25**
26	27	28	29	30	**31**	

November
M	T	W	T	F	**S**	**S**
						1
2	3	4	5	6	**7**	**8**
9	10	11	12	13	**14**	**15**
16	17	18	19	20	**21**	**22**
23	24	25	26	27	**28**	**29**
30						

December
M	T	W	T	F	**S**	**S**
	1	2	3	4	**5**	**6**
7	8	9	10	11	**12**	**13**
14	15	16	17	18	**19**	**20**
21	22	23	24	25	**26**	**27**
28	29	30	31			

2021

January
M	T	W	T	F	**S**	**S**
				1	**2**	**3**
4	5	6	7	8	**9**	**10**
11	12	13	14	15	**16**	**17**
18	19	20	21	22	**23**	**24**
25	26	27	28	29	**30**	**31**

February
M	T	W	T	F	**S**	**S**
1	2	3	4	5	**6**	**7**
8	9	10	11	12	**13**	**14**
15	16	17	18	19	**20**	**21**
22	23	24	25	26	**27**	**28**

March
M	T	W	T	F	**S**	**S**
1	2	3	4	5	**6**	**7**
8	9	10	11	12	**13**	**14**
15	16	17	18	19	**20**	**21**
22	23	24	25	26	**27**	**28**
29	30	31				

April
M	T	W	T	F	**S**	**S**
			1	2	**3**	**4**
5	6	7	8	9	**10**	**11**
12	13	14	15	16	**17**	**18**
19	20	21	22	23	**24**	**25**
26	27	28	29	30		

May
M	T	W	T	F	**S**	**S**
					1	**2**
3	4	5	6	7	**8**	**9**
10	11	12	13	14	**15**	**16**
17	18	19	20	21	**22**	**23**
24	25	26	27	28	**29**	**30**
31						

June
M	T	W	T	F	**S**	**S**
	1	2	3	4	**5**	**6**
7	8	9	10	11	**12**	**13**
14	15	16	17	18	**19**	**20**
21	22	23	24	25	**26**	**27**
28	29	30				

July
M	T	W	T	F	**S**	**S**
			1	2	**3**	**4**
5	6	7	8	9	**10**	**11**
12	13	14	15	16	**17**	**18**
19	20	21	22	23	**24**	**25**
26	27	28	29	30	**31**	

August
M	T	W	T	F	**S**	**S**
						1
2	3	4	5	6	**7**	**8**
9	10	11	12	13	**14**	**15**
16	17	18	19	20	**21**	**22**
23	24	25	26	27	**28**	**29**
30	31					

September
M	T	W	T	F	**S**	**S**
	1	2	3	4	**4**	**5**
6	7	8	9	10	**11**	**12**
13	14	15	16	17	**18**	**19**
20	21	22	23	24	**25**	**26**
27	28	29	30			

October
M	T	W	T	F	**S**	**S**
				1	**2**	**3**
4	5	6	7	8	**9**	**10**
11	12	13	14	15	**16**	**17**
18	19	20	21	22	**23**	**24**
25	26	27	28	29	**30**	**31**

November
M	T	W	T	F	**S**	**S**
1	2	3	4	5	**6**	**7**
8	9	10	11	12	**13**	**14**
15	16	17	18	19	**20**	**21**
22	23	24	25	26	**27**	**28**
29	30					

December
M	T	W	T	F	**S**	**S**
		1	2	3	**4**	**5**
6	7	8	9	10	**11**	**12**
13	14	15	16	17	**18**	**19**
20	21	22	23	24	**25**	**26**
27	28	29	30	31		

2022

January
M	T	W	T	F	**S**	**S**
					1	**2**
3	4	5	6	7	**8**	**9**
10	11	12	13	14	**15**	**16**
17	18	19	20	21	**22**	**23**
24	25	26	27	28	**29**	**30**
31						

February
M	T	W	T	F	**S**	**S**
	1	2	3	4	**5**	**6**
7	8	9	10	11	**12**	**13**
14	15	16	17	18	**19**	**20**
21	22	23	24	25	**26**	**27**
28						

March
M	T	W	T	F	**S**	**S**
	1	2	3	4	**5**	**6**
7	8	9	10	11	**12**	**13**
14	15	16	17	18	**19**	**20**
21	22	23	24	25	**26**	**27**
28	29	30	31			

April
M	T	W	T	F	**S**	**S**
				1	**2**	**3**
4	5	6	7	8	**9**	**10**
11	12	13	14	15	**16**	**17**
18	19	20	21	22	**23**	**24**
25	26	27	28	29	**30**	

May
M	T	W	T	F	**S**	**S**
						1
2	3	4	5	6	**7**	**8**
9	10	11	12	13	**14**	**15**
16	17	18	19	20	**21**	**22**
23	24	25	26	27	**28**	**29**
30	31					

June
M	T	W	T	F	**S**	**S**
		1	2	3	**4**	**5**
6	7	8	9	10	**11**	**12**
13	14	15	16	17	**18**	**19**
20	21	22	23	24	**25**	**26**
27	28	29	30			

July
M	T	W	T	F	**S**	**S**
				1	**2**	**3**
4	5	6	7	8	**9**	**10**
11	12	13	14	15	**16**	**17**
18	19	20	21	22	**23**	**24**
25	26	27	28	29	**30**	**31**

August
M	T	W	T	F	**S**	**S**
1	2	3	4	5	**6**	**7**
8	9	10	11	12	**13**	**14**
15	16	17	18	19	**20**	**21**
22	23	24	25	26	**27**	**28**
29	30	31				

September
M	T	W	T	F	**S**	**S**
			1	2	**3**	**4**
5	6	7	8	9	**10**	**11**
12	13	14	15	16	**17**	**18**
19	20	21	22	23	**24**	**25**
26	27	28	29	30		

October
M	T	W	T	F	**S**	**S**
					1	**2**
3	4	5	6	7	**8**	**9**
10	11	12	13	14	**15**	**16**
17	18	19	20	21	**22**	**23**
24	25	26	27	28	**29**	**30**
31						

November
M	T	W	T	F	**S**	**S**
	1	2	3	4	**5**	**6**
7	8	9	10	11	**12**	**13**
14	15	16	17	18	**19**	**20**
21	22	23	24	25	**26**	**27**
28	29	30				

December
M	T	W	T	F	**S**	**S**
			1	2	**3**	**4**
5	6	7	8	9	**10**	**11**
12	13	14	15	16	**17**	**18**
19	20	21	22	23	**24**	**25**
26	27	28	29	30	**31**	

14 **Monday**

15 **Tuesday**

16 **Wednesday**

17 **Thursday**

18 **Friday**

19 **Saturday**

20 **Sunday**

December 2020

21 **Monday**   Winter Solstice (shortest day)

22 **Tuesday**

23 **Wednesday**

24 **Thursday** Christmas Eve

25 **Friday** Christmas Day (Bank Holiday)

26 **Saturday** Boxing Day

27 **Sunday**

January 2021

Jaguar Mk I/II

The question anyone might reasonably ask while drooling over the lithe, chrome-encrusted and leather-lined Jaguar Mk II in our illustration, is: 'What about the Mk I?'

There is no Mk I, of course. That's a retrospective title applied to the Jaguar 2.4-litre, introduced in 1955 – the first Jaguar with unitary-construction instead of a separate chassis.

It looked rather slug-like with its tapering tail and 'spats' sealing the rear wheels (4in closer together than the fronts) into the bodywork. It had sporty handling but was fairly heavy and, because of that, its engine felt gutless. Stung into reaction, Jaguar created a 3.4-litre rendition, effectively installing the power unit from its D-type racer. It could manage 120mph, sensational in 1957, but 210bhp through a narrow back axle together with drum brakes made for a frightening machine if driven hard.

None of which should have boded well for Jaguar. Yet the Mk II revealed

in 1959 sorted the drawbacks and emerged as an unlikely all-time great.

The fundamental handling problems were fixed with a widened rear track, new back axle, revised suspension and standard disc brakes all round. Meanwhile, a masterful facelift produced slimmer roof pillars and larger, more graceful windows.

The company felt confident enough to offer a 3.8-litre engine too, conjuring up the ultimate 1960s sports saloon, a blistering 125mph performer. Renamed 240 and 340 (the 3.8 was axed) in 1967, the cars survived two more years.

Month **Planner**

Friday 1	Saturday 2	Sunday 3	Monday 4	Tuesday 5	Wednesday 6	Thursday 7	Friday 8	Saturday 9	Sunday 10	Monday 11	Tuesday 12	Wednesday 13	Thursday 14	Friday 15	Saturda 16

Sunday	Monday	Tuesday	Wednesday	Thursday	Friday	Saturday	Sunday	Monday	Tuesday	Wednesday	Thursday	Friday	Saturday	Sunday
17	18	19	20	21	22	23	24	25	26	27	28	29	30	31

December 2020**/January** 2021

28 **Monday**   Boxing Day Bank Holiday

29 **Tuesday**

30 **Wednesday**

31 **Thursday**   New Year's Eve

1 **Friday**   New Year's Day (Bank Holiday)

2 **Saturday**

3 **Sunday**

4 **Monday**	Bank Holiday (Scotland)	

5 **Tuesday**

6 **Wednesday**

7 Thursday

8 Friday

9 Saturday

10 Sunday

11 **Monday**

12 **Tuesday**

13 **Wednesday**

14 **Thursday**

15 **Friday**

16 **Saturday**

17 **Sunday**

18 **Monday**

19 **Tuesday**

20 **Wednesday**

21 **Thursday**

22 **Friday**

23 **Saturday**

24 **Sunday**

January 2021

25 **Monday**

26 **Tuesday**

27 **Wednesday**

28 | **Thursday**

29 | **Friday**

30 | **Saturday**

31 | **Sunday**

Month **Planner**

Monday	Tuesday	Wednesday	Thursday	Friday	Saturday	Sunday	Monday	Tuesday	Wednesday	Thursday	Friday	Saturday	Sunday	Monday	Tuesday
1	2	3	4	5	6	7	8	9	10	11	12	13	14	15	16

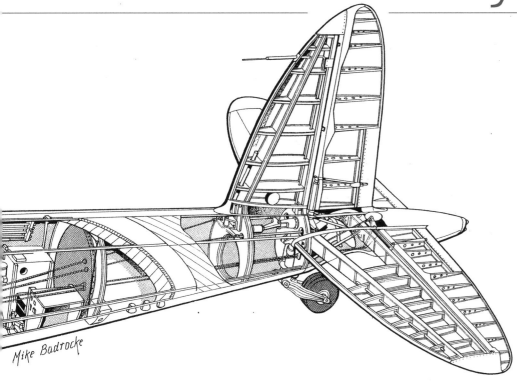

Mike Badrocke

de Havilland Mosquito B XVI

With its slippery lines and crackling snarl from its twin Rolls-Royce Merlin engines, the de Havilland Mosquito looked and sounded as though it meant business. And it did. When it went into service with the RAF in 1941 this charismatic and devastatingly effective British warbird could show a clean pair of heels to everything else in the air, whether fighter or bomber, Allied or Axis. It became a jack of all trades and master of them all, and as such became the most versatile multi-role combat aircraft ever built.

Never hidebound by convention, the de Havilland company's original design idea was fresh and simple, but baffling to the British Air Ministry: a speed bomber built from wood with no armament. It seemed laughable. But de Havilland had the last laugh, for the 'Wooden Wonder' went on to define the concept of multi-role combat aircraft in the Second World War.

Thanks to its wooden structure, hundreds of trades outside the aviation industry played a vital role in the Mosquito's construction as parts were subcontracted all over the country – trades which would otherwise be making no contribution to the war effort, such as furniture makers.

The 'Mossie' found roles in every aerial theatre of war, roles that it fulfilled superlatively, from fast bomber to night-fighter, pathfinder, high-speed photo-reconnaissance, weather reporting, fighter-bomber, intruder – and even as an airliner for BOAC. It could fly at great altitude in safety from attack, it could sneak fast and low under enemy radar, it discovered V-weapon sites, it carried the Barnes Wallis Highball bomb (albeit not in anger), and took part in a number of high-profile operations. As well as the RAF, it served with the Royal Canadian Air Force, the Royal Australian Air Force, the US Army Air Force, and more than 12 other air forces, all of whom recognised its outstanding capabilities.

Wednesday	Thursday	Friday	Saturday	Sunday	Monday	Tuesday	Wednesday	Thursday	Friday	Saturday	Sunday
17	18	19	20	21	22	23	24	25	26	27	28

February 2021

1 Monday

2 Tuesday

3 Wednesday

4 **Thursday**

5 **Friday**

6 **Saturday**

7 **Sunday**

February 2021

8 Monday

9 Tuesday

10 Wednesday

11 **Thursday**

12 **Friday**

13 **Saturday**

14 **Sunday**   St Valentine's Day

15 **Monday**

16 **Tuesday**   Shrove Tuesday

17 **Wednesday**

18 **Thursday**

19 **Friday**

20 **Saturday**

21 **Sunday**

February 2021

22 **Monday**

23 **Tuesday**

24 **Wednesday**

25 **Thursday**

26 **Friday**

27 **Saturday**

28 **Sunday**

March 2021

Citroën GS

Month Planner

Monday	Tuesday	Wednesday	Thursday	Friday	Saturday	Sunday	Monday	Tuesday	Wednesday	Thursday	Friday	Saturday	Sunday	Monday	Tuesday
1	2	3	4	5	6	7	8	9	10	11	12	13	14	15	16

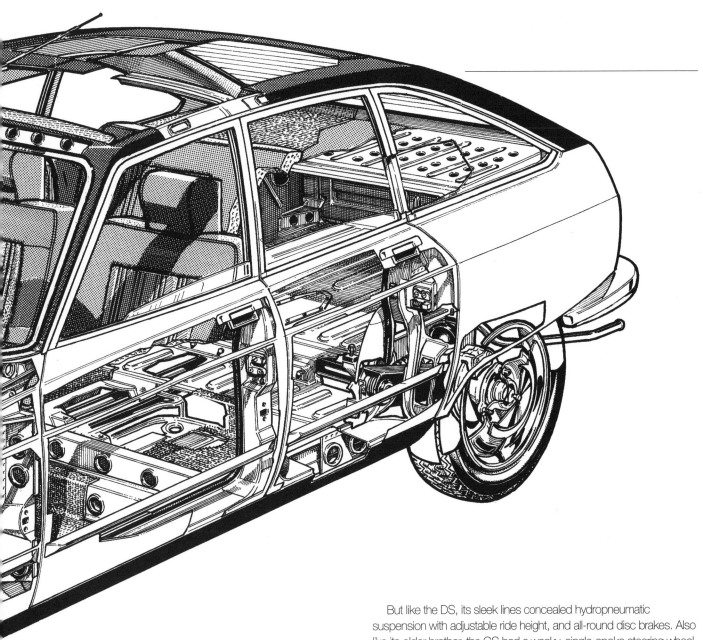

Medium-sized family cars got a whole lot more adventurous in 1970 after Citroën took the wraps off its aerodynamic GS. It was very much the Toyota Prius of its time, bristling with interesting technological features yet aimed at those who perhaps valued comfort and economy above ultimate performance.

The GS, in fact, filled the yawning chasm between the little Dyane and Ami models and the shark-like DS, and mixed the iconic features of both. Like the Dyane, the GS featured a horizontally opposed, air-cooled engine, albeit an all-new unit with four cylinders instead of two.

But like the DS, its sleek lines concealed hydropneumatic suspension with adjustable ride height, and all-round disc brakes. Also like its older brother, the GS had a wacky, single-spoke steering wheel.

Relatively meagre luggage accommodation (there was no hatchback until the replacement GSA arrived in 1979) was made up for by the capacious GS estate introduced in 1972, and levels of trim ranged from the plain Confort to the leather-rich Pallas.

With its exceptionally smooth ride, fine roadholding and roomy cabin, the GS was a multi-faceted car bound to inspire pride in any technologically minded owner. For more conventional British buyers, though, it was largely viewed with suspicion, and wasn't a popular choice as a used car, leading to a rapid dwindling of GSs on UK roads during the 1980s.

Wednesday	Thursday	Friday	Saturday	Sunday	Monday	Tuesday	Wednesday	Thursday	Friday	Saturday	Sunday	Monday	Tuesday	Wednesday
17	18	19	20	21	22	23	24	25	26	27	28	29	30	31

1 Monday

2 Tuesday

3 Wednesday

MAR

4 Thursday

5 Friday

6 Saturday

7 Sunday

MAR

8 **Monday**

9 **Tuesday**

10 **Wednesday**

11 Thursday

12 Friday

13 Saturday

14 Sunday

Mothering Sunday

MAR

15 Monday

16 Tuesday

17 Wednesday

St Patrick's Day (Ireland)

18 **Thursday**

19 **Friday**

20 **Saturday** Spring Equinox

21 **Sunday**

MAR

22 **Monday**

23 **Tuesday**

24 **Wednesday**

25 **Thursday**

26 **Friday**

27 **Saturday**

28 **Sunday**   British Summer Time begins / Palm Sunday

April 2021

International Space Station

With a total mass of around 450 metric tonnes and a width of more than 350ft (108m), the International Space Station (ISS) is the biggest structure ever placed in orbit around the Earth. It took 13 years to build, using the combined resources of 15 countries, together with the skill and expertise accumulated in more than 40 years of space exploration. This massive complex emerged from the competition of the Cold War into a new Space Age of cooperation. Arguably mankind's biggest engineering achievement of the Space Age.

The ISS is the world's first truly international space-based laboratory, providing research facilities for scientists, engineers and entrepreneurs in government, industry and in the privately owned commercial sector. Dedicated to non-military activities, it provides an open resource for specialists from many disciplines in which to live and work, and from which to conduct research.

The project partners (USA, Russia, Japan, Europe and Canada) are pledged to continue providing those facilities for a sustained programme of research and discovery involving new medicines, better semiconductor materials, more efficient ways of making exotic metals, and carrying out research in areas where new knowledge is being gathered every day. As an inspiration for school children and students everywhere, it has value for the next generation of scientists, engineers, physicians and geographers, and astronomers and chemists.

Month **Planner**

Thursday	Friday	Saturday	Sunday	Monday	Tuesday	Wednesday	Thursday	Friday	Saturday	Sunday	Monday	Tuesday	Wednesday	Thursday	Friday
1	2	3	4	5	6	7	8	9	10	11	12	13	14	15	16

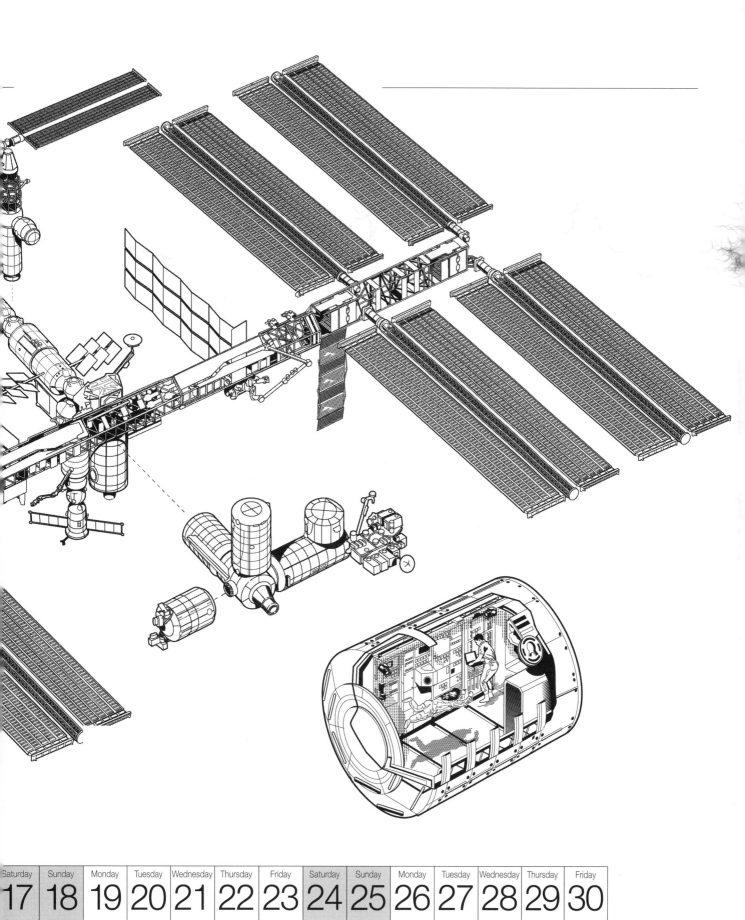

Saturday	Sunday	Monday	Tuesday	Wednesday	Thursday	Friday	Saturday	Sunday	Monday	Tuesday	Wednesday	Thursday	Friday
17	18	19	20	21	22	23	24	25	26	27	28	29	30

MAR

29 **Monday**

30 **Tuesday**

31 **Wednesday**

1   **Thursday**   Maundy Thursday

2   **Friday**   Good Friday (Bank Holiday)

3   **Saturday**

4   **Sunday**   Easter Sunday

5 Monday

Easter Monday (Bank Holiday, not Scotland)

6 Tuesday

7 Wednesday

8 **Thursday**

9 **Friday**

10 **Saturday**

11 **Sunday**

12 **Monday**

13 **Tuesday**

14 **Wednesday**

15 **Thursday**

16 **Friday**

17 **Saturday**

18 **Sunday**

19 **Monday**

20 **Tuesday**

21 **Wednesday**

22 **Thursday**

23 **Friday** St George's Day (England)

24 **Saturday**

25 **Sunday**

May 2021

Mercedes-Benz
250/280SL

Month **Planner**

Saturday	Sunday	Monday	Tuesday	Wednesday	Thursday	Friday	Saturday	Sunday	Monday	Tuesday	Wednesday	Thursday	Friday	Saturday	Sunday
1	2	3	4	5	6	7	8	9	10	11	12	13	14	15	16

Never mind engine oil; most cars need gallons of metaphorical moisturiser to stop them feeling dated after even 10 years, much less 40. Looked at like this, the so-called 'Pagoda-roof' Mercedes-Benz SL is startlingly wrinkle-free. There's barely a crow's foot on its urbane and handsome visage. Its road manners are nostalgia-tinged contemporary, and it has marvellous, Jaguar-shaming build quality.

The 1963 230SL replaced the race-bred 300SL and the pretty, if gutless, 190SL in one fell swoop. The 2.3-litre, six-cylinder, fuel-injected engine offered a fiery 150bhp. Thanks to an abnormally wide track, well sorted suspension, fat tyres and a ground-hugging stance, its handling and roadholding were fantastic. It could also do 120mph … and yet cost double the price of a 150mph Jaguar E-type.

A wide grille, stacked headlights and flared wheelarches were massaged into an elegant shape, while the layered bumpers, chrome bedecked dashboard, ivory steering wheel and hubcaps matched to the bodywork colour oozed cachet. Every SL came with its own detachable metal hardtop. Unusually, Merc offered its excellent automatic gearbox on the SL and, with this available, few people opted for the notchy manual.

Progressively larger engines, first in the rare 1966 250SL and then in the 1968 280SL, gave the car enhanced cruising prowess. Softer suspension and better refinement made it feel more luxurious, and four-wheel disc brakes were now on hand should panic stations strike.

Monday	Tuesday	Wednesday	Thursday	Friday	Saturday	Sunday	Monday	Tuesday	Wednesday	Thursday	Friday	Saturday	Sunday	Monday
17	18	19	20	21	22	23	24	25	26	27	28	29	30	31

26 **Monday**

27 **Tuesday**

28 **Wednesday**

29 **Thursday** 🕐

30 **Friday**

1 **Saturday**

2 **Sunday**

3 **Monday**

Early May Bank Holiday

4 **Tuesday**

5 **Wednesday**

6 **Thursday**

7 **Friday**

8 **Saturday**

9 **Sunday**

May 2021

10 **Monday**

11 **Tuesday**

12 **Wednesday**

13 Thursday

14 Friday

15 Saturday

16 Sunday

MAY

17 Monday

18 Tuesday

19 Wednesday

20 **Thursday**

21 **Friday**

22 **Saturday**

23 **Sunday**

May 2021

24 **Monday**

25 **Tuesday**

26 **Wednesday**

27 Thursday

28 Friday

29 Saturday

30 Sunday

June 2021

Leopard 1 Main Battle Tank

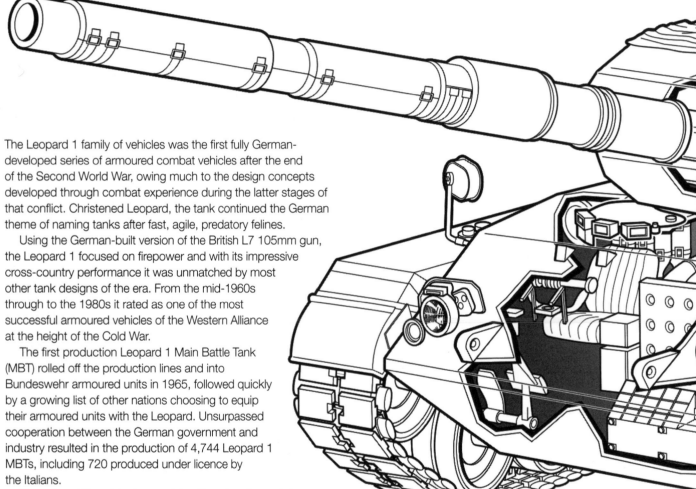

The Leopard 1 family of vehicles was the first fully German-developed series of armoured combat vehicles after the end of the Second World War, owing much to the design concepts developed through combat experience during the latter stages of that conflict. Christened Leopard, the tank continued the German theme of naming tanks after fast, agile, predatory felines.

Using the German-built version of the British L7 105mm gun, the Leopard 1 focused on firepower and with its impressive cross-country performance it was unmatched by most other tank designs of the era. From the mid-1960s through to the 1980s it rated as one of the most successful armoured vehicles of the Western Alliance at the height of the Cold War.

The first production Leopard 1 Main Battle Tank (MBT) rolled off the production lines and into Bundeswehr armoured units in 1965, followed quickly by a growing list of other nations choosing to equip their armoured units with the Leopard. Unsurpassed cooperation between the German government and industry resulted in the production of 4,744 Leopard 1 MBTs, including 720 produced under licence by the Italians.

The adaptability of the Leopard 1 rolling chassis made it an ideal base upon which to develop a wide range of special-purpose vehicles. New-build variants, including anti-aircraft, recovery, obstacle breaching and engineering examples, totalled 1,628 vehicles, with many more converted from earlier-model MBT hulls. While the majority were supplied to the Bundeswehr, the Leopard 1 family was also purchased by nine other countries, with a further eight nations acquiring refurbished or converted vehicles from the original inventory.

The last Leopard 1s were finally retired in 2003 after 38 years of service with the German Bundeswehr, succeeded by the Leopard 2 as the Main Battle Tank of the German Army. However, it remains in use in noteworthy numbers in southern Europe and South America as an MBT.

Month **Planner**

Tuesday	Wednesday	Thursday	Friday	Saturday	Sunday	Monday	Tuesday	Wednesday	Thursday	Friday	Saturday	Sunday	Monday	Tuesday	Wednesda
1	2	3	4	5	6	7	8	9	10	11	12	13	14	15	16

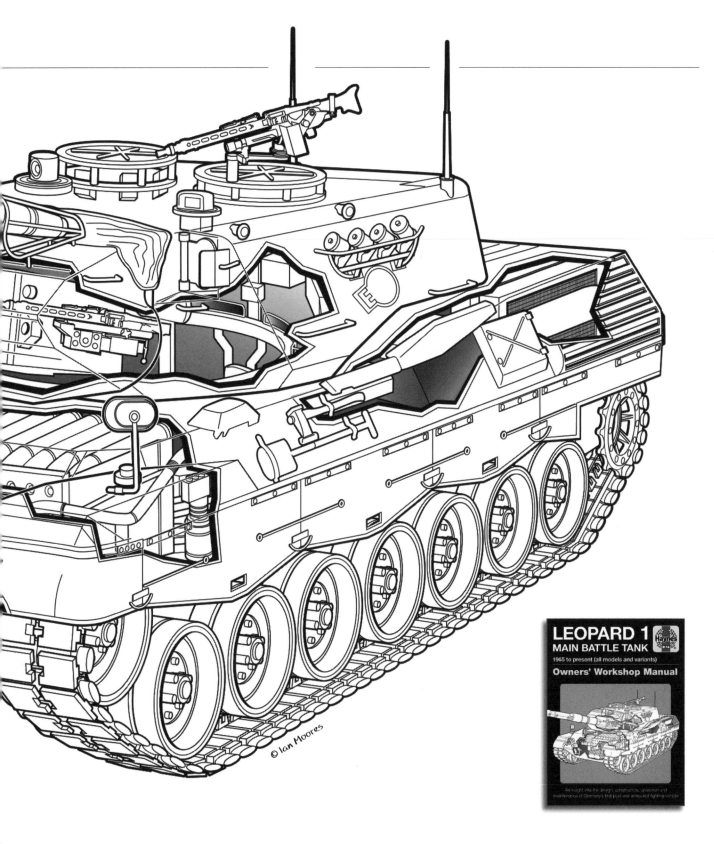

© Ian Moores

LEOPARD 1 Haynes
MAIN BATTLE TANK
1965 to present (all models and variants)
Owners' Workshop Manual

Thursday	Friday	Saturday	Sunday	Monday	Tuesdsay	Wednesday	Thursday	Friday	Saturday	Sunday	Monday	Tuesdsay	Wednesday
17	18	19	20	21	22	23	24	25	26	27	28	29	30

31 **Monday**   Spring Bank Holiday

1 **Tuesday**

2 **Wednesday**

3 **Thursday**

4 **Friday**

5 **Saturday**

6 **Sunday**

7 **Monday**

8 **Tuesday**

9 **Wednesday**

10 **Thursday**

11 **Friday**

12 **Saturday**

13 **Sunday**

14 **Monday** 🕐

15 **Tuesday**

16 **Wednesday**

17 **Thursday**

18 **Friday**

19 **Saturday**

20 **Sunday**   Father's Day (UK)

21 **Monday**   Summer Solstice (longest day)

22 **Tuesday**

23 **Wednesday**

24 **Thursday**

25 **Friday**

26 **Saturday**

27 **Sunday**

July 2021

MG Midget Mk3

With this car in 1961, MG – pioneer of the mass-produced sports car – had become a badge on the Austin-Healey Sprite, with all its virtues and shortcomings. The Midget was not for competing at traffic light stand-offs – more for winding its burbling way down secondary roads with the top down.

As on the Sprite, the engine was enlarged from 948 to 1,098cc in late 1962, and by 1964 the Mk2 Midget had gained a taller windscreen, wind-up windows and door locks, semi-elliptical rear springs and an extra 3bhp. In 1966 came the Mk3, with a 1,275cc 65bhp engine and a permanently attached hood to replaced the rather flimsy canvas and tube affair of the early cars.

Top speed improved by only 2mph, but it gave more mid-range power that really meant the Midget's undeniable driving fun could be fully exploited. In 1969 came a comprehensive cosmetic makeover, including rounded rear wheelarches and trendy Rostyle wheels, and sales continued apace despite the little roadster's creaking design.

Indeed, the Midget got yet another new lease of life four years later when, to keep the car saleable in the USA, it was bestowed with prominent plastic bumpers, an increased ride height to meet Stateside safety laws, and the 1,493cc Triumph Spitfire engine and gearbox which could meet emissions laws. The Midget continued in production until 1979.

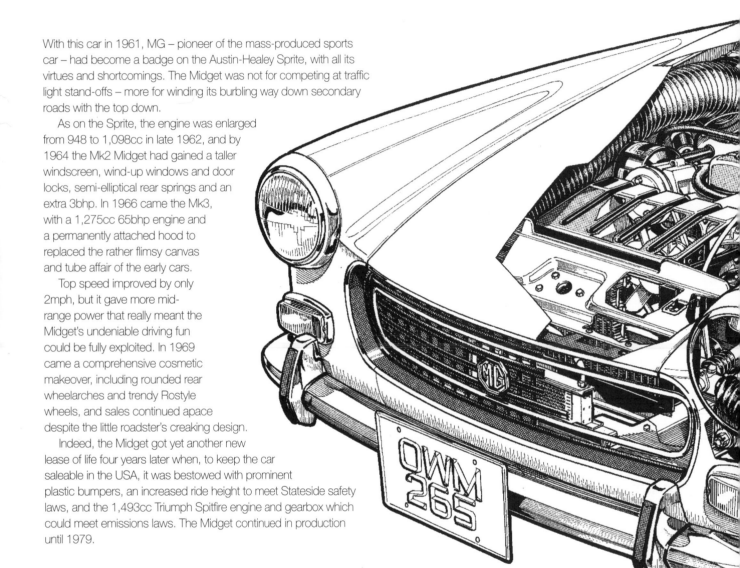

Month Planner

Thursday	Friday	Saturday	Sunday	Monday	Tuesday	Wednesday	Thursday	Friday	Saturday	Sunday	Monday	Tuesday	Wednesday	Thursday	Friday
1	2	3	4	5	6	7	8	9	10	11	12	13	14	15	16

Saturday	Sunday	Monday	Tuesday	Wednesday	Thursday	Friday	Saturday	Sunday	Monday	Tuesday	Wednesday	Thursday	Friday	Saturday
17	18	19	20	21	22	23	24	25	26	27	28	29	30	31

28 **Monday**

29 **Tuesday**

30 **Wednesday**

1 **Thursday**

2 **Friday**

3 **Saturday**

4 **Sunday**

5 **Monday**

6 **Tuesday**

7 **Wednesday**

8 **Thursday**

9 **Friday**

10 **Saturday**

11 **Sunday**

July 2021

12	**Monday**	Holiday (Battle of the Boyne) (NI only)

13	**Tuesday**

14	**Wednesday**

15 Thursday

🕐

16 Friday

17 Saturday

18 Sunday

19 **Monday**

20 **Tuesday**

21 **Wednesday**

22 **Thursday** 🕐

23 **Friday**

24 **Saturday**

25 **Sunday**

Month **Planner**

Sunday	Monday	Tuesday	Wednesday	Thursday	Friday	Saturday	Sunday	Monday	Tuesday	Wednesday	Thursday	Friday	Saturday	Sunday	Monday
1	2	3	4	5	6	7	8	9	10	11	12	13	14	15	16

August 2021

London Underground

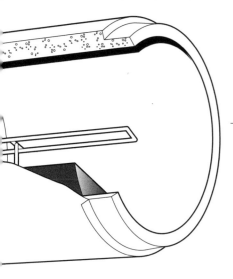

The London Underground, or Tube, is the world's oldest subterranean rail network, having been in continuous use for over 150 years, and remains one of its largest and busiest.

No other undergound system in the world displays such a huge variety of station styles, ranging from the earliest surviving Victorian brick buildings, via the steel-framed faience-tile-clad stations of the Edwardian era and the classic 'moderne' stations of the 1930s, through to the steel and glass structures of today.

As steam gave way to electric traction, a handful of tremendously talented men steered the Underground to a pre-war level of excellence that was envied around the world. The stylish trains were designed and built to very high standards, together with their stations and information graphics, all underlined by a remarkable quality of service. The Underground's engineers had always grasped the potential of technology for the convenience of passengers, automatic ticket dispensing machines being an example.

The challenges faced in the immediate post-war years of austerity led to the ground-breaking Victoria Line of the 1960s, which introduced Automatic Train Control (a world first) and a first attempt at automatic fare collection. The journey then continued to the remarkable Jubilee Line Extension, and there will be equally innovative future developments.

The continuous evolution of the Underground demonstrates that ever-increasing passenger demands means that it can never afford to stand still!

Tuesday	Wednesday	Thursday	Friday	Saturday	Sunday	Monday	Tuesday	Wednesday	Thursday	Friday	Saturday	Sunday	Monday	Tuesday
17	18	19	20	21	22	23	24	25	26	27	28	29	30	31

26 **Monday**

27 **Tuesday**

28 **Wednesday**

29 **Thursday** 🕐

30 **Friday**

31 **Saturday**

1 **Sunday**

2 **Monday**   Summer Bank Holiday (Scotland)

3 **Tuesday**

4 **Wednesday**

5 **Thursday**

6 **Friday**

7 **Saturday**

8 **Sunday**

9 **Monday**

10 **Tuesday**

11 **Wednesday**

12 **Thursday**

13 **Friday**

14 **Saturday**

15 **Sunday**

16 **Monday**

17 **Tuesday**

18 **Wednesday**

19 **Thursday**

20 **Friday**

21 **Saturday**

22 **Sunday**

23 **Monday**

24 **Tuesday**

25 **Wednesday**

26 **Thursday**

27 **Friday**

28 **Saturday**

29 **Sunday**

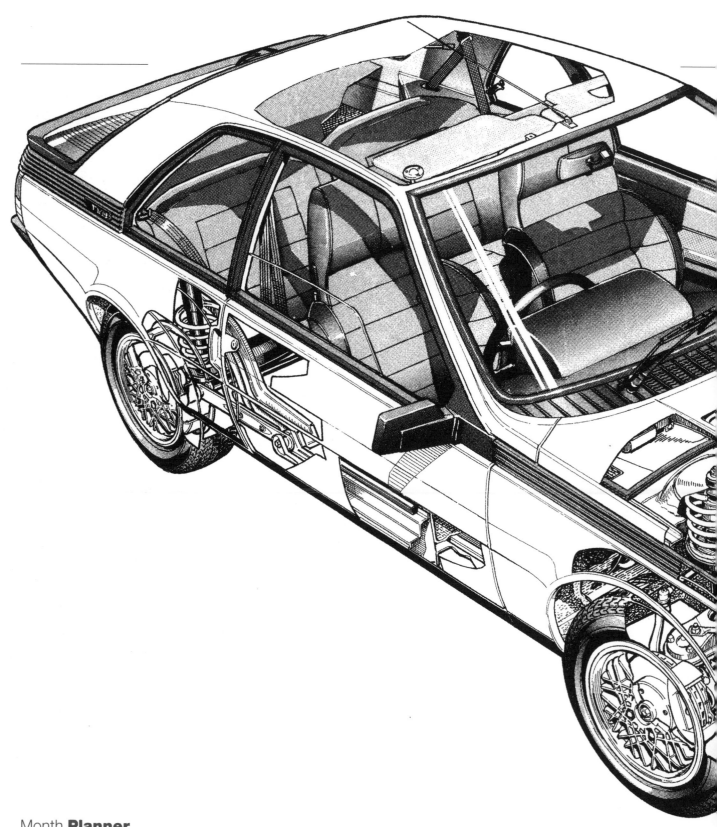

Month **Planner**

Wednesday	Thursday	Friday	Saturday	Sunday	Monday	Tuesday	Wednesday	Thursday	Friday	Saturday	Sunday	Monday	Tuesday	Wednesday	Thursday
1	2	3	4	5	6	7	8	9	10	11	12	13	14	15	16

Renault Fuego

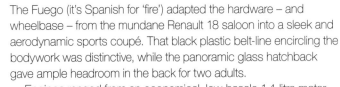

The Fuego (it's Spanish for 'fire') adapted the hardware – and wheelbase – from the mundane Renault 18 saloon into a sleek and aerodynamic sports coupé. That black plastic belt-line encircling the bodywork was distinctive, while the panoramic glass hatchback gave ample headroom in the back for two adults.

Engines ranged from an economical, low-hassle 1.4-litre motor developing 64bhp up to a 110bhp 2-litre. But in 1984 Renault also produced the Fuego Turbo, with a blown 1.6-litre engine putting out 132bhp through the front wheels; the torque-steer was almost as obscene as the huge stickers on the doors reading 'TURBO', for the benefit of anyone who hadn't already twigged.

Nor was the turbo the most interesting engine. A year before, Renault slotted the 18's 2.1-litre turbo-diesel into the Fuego. With 88bhp, it was a modest performer, but is more significant for being the first vaguely sporting car with diesel power.

And the innovations didn't stop there, either. In the electronic spirit of the early 1980s, the Fuego was the first car with a remote central locking system.

In truth, the car was not the committed performance driver's choice. The spongy MacPherson strut suspension, betraying the Renault 18 within, had been devised for comfort rather than agility. However, on smooth, straight roads, the Fuego's stability and ride was excellent, probably thanks also to a low drag factor of just 0.34.

Friday	Saturday	Sunday	Monday	Tuesday	Wednesday	Thursday	Friday	Saturday	Sunday	Monday	Tuesday	Wednesday	Thursday
17	18	19	20	21	22	23	24	25	26	27	28	29	30

30 **Monday** Summer Bank Holiday (not Scotland)

31 **Tuesday**

1 **Wednesday**

2 **Thursday**

3 **Friday**

4 **Saturday**

5 **Sunday**

6 **Monday**

7 **Tuesday**

8 **Wednesday**

9 **Thursday**

10 **Friday**

11 **Saturday**

12 **Sunday**

13 **Monday**

14 **Tuesday**

15 **Wednesday**

16 **Thursday**

17 **Friday**

18 **Saturday**

19 **Sunday**

20 **Monday**

21 **Tuesday**

22 **Wednesday**   Autumn Equinox

23 **Thursday**

24 **Friday**

25 **Saturday**

26 **Sunday**

October 2021

Astronaut

The role of astronaut is no longer simply about the heroic explorer braving unknown dangers in the cosmos. It has been the basis of a professional career for more than 500 men and women since Yuri Gagarin became the first human to enter space in 1961.

Astronauts have to go through a rigorous recruitment procedure and training programme before travelling and living in space. A typical mission to and from the International Space Station (ISS) starts with a thrilling launch, then orbital rendezvous and docking. Life aboard the ISS is a high-intensity working trip crammed full of scientific experiments, maintenance tasks, and a strict exercise regime to counter bodily deterioration. This all takes place in the extraordinary environment of weightlessness, while an addictive and constantly changing panorama of Earth unfolds from the windows. Return to Earth involves a fiery re-entry inside a small capsule, descent by parachute and a bumpy landing with retro-rockets on the vast plains of the steppes, or a splash-down in the ocean.

Afterwards, the long process of re-adapting to Earth's gravity begins. And what does the retired astronaut do when space flight is over? Coping with fame has been an issue for some, while many have gone into careers in education, business, engineering and, inspired by their views of the cosmos, art.

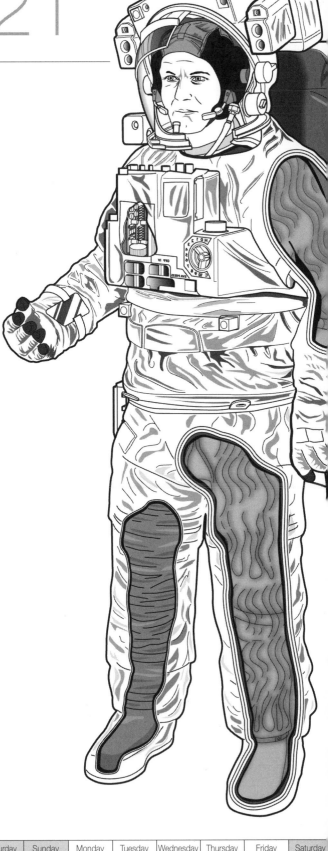

Month **Planner**

Friday	Saturday	Sunday	Monday	Tuesday	Wednesday	Thursday	Friday	Saturday	Sunday	Monday	Tuesday	Wednesday	Thursday	Friday	Saturday
1	2	3	4	5	6	7	8	9	10	11	12	13	14	15	16

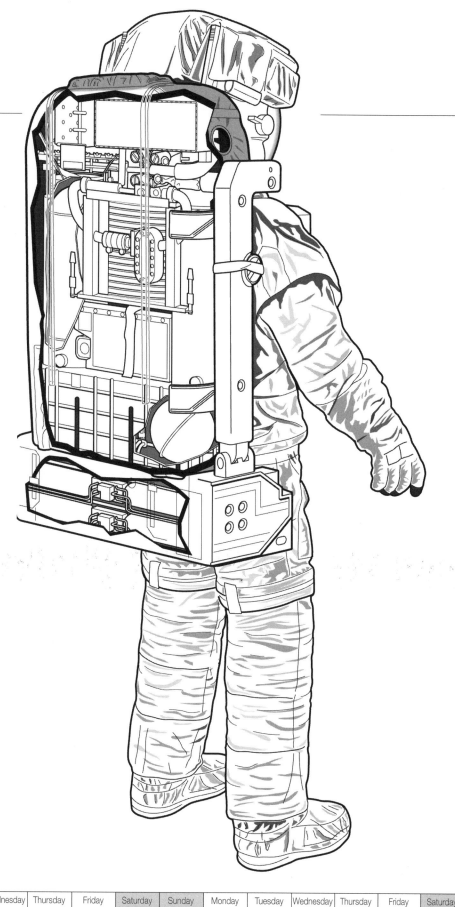

Sunday	Monday	Tuesday	Wednesday	Thursday	Friday	Saturday	Sunday	Monday	Tuesday	Wednesday	Thursday	Friday	Saturday	Sunday
17	18	19	20	21	22	23	24	25	26	27	28	29	30	31

27 **Monday**

28 **Tuesday**

29 **Wednesday**

30 **Thursday**

1 **Friday**

2 **Saturday**

3 **Sunday**

4 Monday

5 Tuesday

6 Wednesday

7 **Thursday**

8 **Friday**

9 **Saturday**

10 **Sunday**

11 Monday

12 Tuesday

13 Wednesday

14 **Thursday**

15 **Friday**

16 **Saturday**

17 **Sunday**

18 **Monday**

19 **Tuesday**

20 **Wednesday**

OCT

21 Thursday

22 Friday

23 Saturday

24 Sunday

25 **Monday**

26 **Tuesday**

27 **Wednesday**

28 Thursday

29 Friday

30 Saturday

31 Sunday

British Summer Time ends

Triumph Spitfire

The dinky Spitfire was based wholesale on Triumph's Herald, which featured an old-fashioned and cheap-to-make separate chassis and bolt-on body panels. Yet the Herald also had artfully detailed bodywork, the work of Italian designer Giovanni Michelotti, and he was brought in again to design the 1962 Spitfire, Triumph's MG Midget rival. A lovely job he did too.

The engine was eager enough to out-run the Midget – good for 90mph with 0–60mph in 16.5sec. Front disc brakes, a decent soft-top and roomy boot made it a practical and fun everyday proposition too. In its roadholding, however, the Spitfire inherited the Herald's flawed swing-axle independent rear suspension, making it twitchy in fast, ill-judged corners.

The 1965 Mk II gained 4bhp from its new 1,296cc engine, and there was 8bhp more for the 1967 Mk III. The Spitfire could now hit the ton, preferably on a dead-straight road. …

In 1970 Triumph revamped the car, giving this MkIV – shown in our artwork – new and more elegant bodywork. Best of all, engineers fettled the rear suspension; they now called it 'swing-spring', and it cured the previously wayward tendencies.

The final change to the car came in 1975 when a 1,500cc engine meeting all American anti-smog rules was standardised. In this ultimate guise, the Spitfire 1500 remained on sale until August 1980, ending an amazing 18-year lifespan.

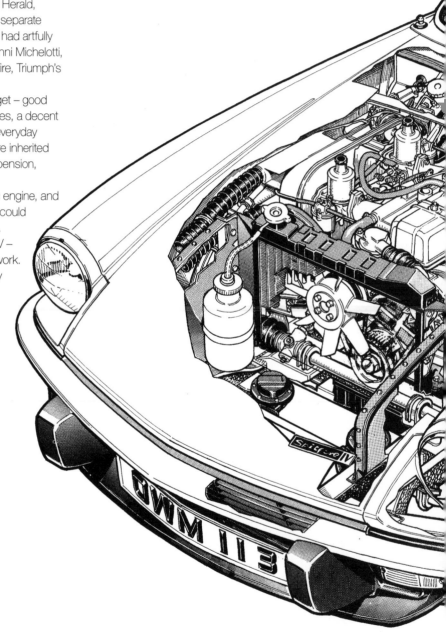

Month **Planner**

Monday	Tuesday	Wednesday	Thursday	Friday	Saturday	Sunday	Monday	Tuesday	Wednesday	Thursday	Friday	Saturday	Sunday	Monday	Tuesday
1	2	3	4	5	6	7	8	9	10	11	12	13	14	15	16

Wednesday	Thursday	Friday	Saturday	Sunday	Monday	Tuesday	Wednesday	Thursday	Friday	Saturday	Sunday	Monday	Tuesday
17	18	19	20	21	22	23	24	25	26	27	28	29	30

1 **Monday**

2 **Tuesday**

3 **Wednesday**

4 Thursday

5 Friday

6 Saturday

7 Sunday

8 **Monday**

9 **Tuesday**

10 **Wednesday**

11 **Thursday**

12 **Friday**

13 **Saturday**

14 **Sunday**   Remembrance Sunday

15 Monday

16 Tuesday

17 Wednesday

18 Thursday

19 Friday

20 Saturday

21 Sunday

22 Monday

23 Tuesday

24 Wednesday

25 **Thursday**

26 **Friday**

27 **Saturday**

28 **Sunday**

NOV

Peugeot 205

The little 205's position as the 11th best-selling single car design of all time is impressive; the acclaim it won during its whole lifetime is extraordinary.

Car magazine, for example, anointed it as the single best car the 1980s produced, while seasoned hacks at rival *Autocar* stated in 1991 it was 'still the best small car' – and that for a lowly 1.1 model tested against Ford's all-new Fiesta. That year, too, the eight-year-old car accounted for 3% of the whole UK market. And, throughout its 15 years on sale, it was never once facelifted.

The neat and timeless Pininfarina styling was certainly a factor in its appeal, but the overall rightness of the 205 won people over – the superbly roomy cabin, thanks to compact torsion bar suspension, the supple ride, the lightness that meant even the smallest engines felt punchy. Perhaps most of all, it was the high-torque XUD7 diesel engine available in the car, a motor so quiet and powerful it single-handedly turned sentiment in favour of small diesels.

Meanwhile, the 205 GTi (depicted in our artwork), with its lowered suspension and widened wheelarches, grabbed the hot hatchback baton from Volkswagen and sprinted with it. Once again, its legacy lingers: the most powerful 1.6-litre edition remains a yardstick of driver satisfaction, acceleration and handling by which modern fun cars are still measured.

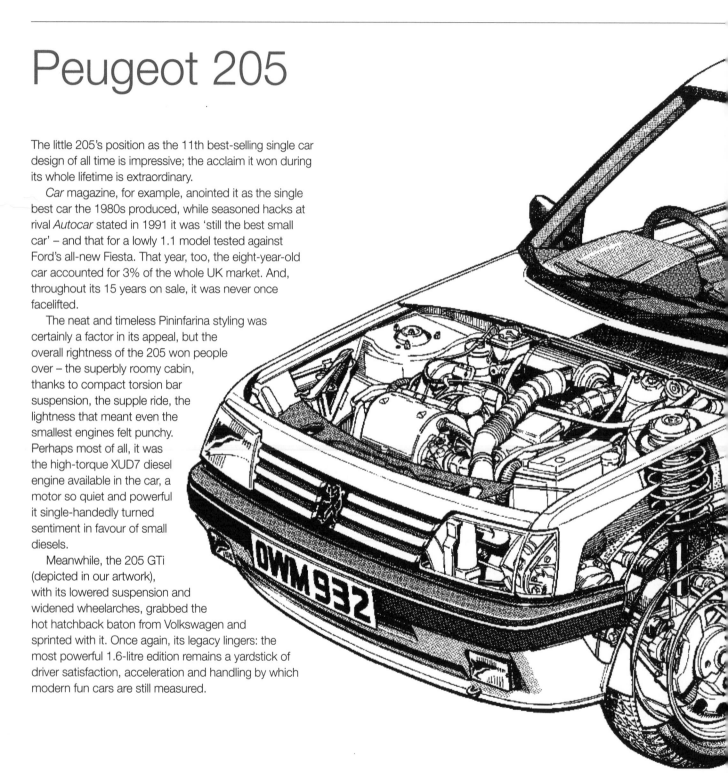

Month **Planner**

Wednesday	Thursday	Friday	Saturday	Sunday	Monday	Tuesday	Wednesday	Thursday	Friday	Saturday	Sunday	Monday	Tuesday	Wednesday	Thursday
1	2	3	4	5	6	7	8	9	10	11	12	13	14	15	16

November/December 2021

29 **Monday**

🕐

30 **Tuesday**

1 **Wednesday**

2 **Thursday**

3 **Friday**

4 **Saturday**

5 **Sunday**

6 **Monday**

7 **Tuesday**

8 **Wednesday**

9 Thursday

10 Friday

11 Saturday

12 Sunday

13 Monday

14 Tuesday

15 Wednesday

16 Thursday

17 Friday

18 Saturday

19 Sunday

20 **Monday**

21 **Tuesday** Winter Solstice (shortest day)

22 **Wednesday**

23 | **Thursday** | 🕐

24 | **Friday** | Christmas Eve

25 | **Saturday** | Christmas Day

26 | **Sunday** | Boxing Day

December 2021

27 **Monday**   (Christmas Day Bank Holiday)

28 **Tuesday**   (Boxing Day Bank Holiday)

29 **Wednesday**

30 **Thursday** 🕐

31 **Friday** New Year's Eve

1 **Saturday** New Year's Day

2 **Sunday**

Appointments **January 2022**

Saturday 1	Monday 17
Sunday **2**	Tuesday 18
Monday 3	Wednesday 19
Tuesday 4	Thursday 20
Wednesday 5	Friday 21
Thursday 6	Saturday 22
Friday 7	**Sunday** **23**
Saturday 8	Monday 24
Sunday **9**	Tuesday 25
Monday 10	Wednesday 26
Tuesday 11	Thursday 27
Wednesday 12	Friday 28
Thursday 13	Saturday 29
Friday 14	**Sunday** **30**
Saturday 15	Monday 31
Sunday **16**	

Appointments **February 2022**

Tuesday 1	Thursday 17
Wednesday 2	Friday 18
Thursday 3	Saturday 19
Friday 4	**Sunday** **20**
Saturday 5	Monday 21
Sunday **6**	Tuesday 22
Monday 7	Wednesday 23
Tuesday 8	Thursday 24
Wednesday 9	Friday 25
Thursday 10	Saturday 26
Friday 11	**Sunday** **27**
Saturday 12	Monday 28
Sunday **13**	
Monday 14	
Tuesday 15	
Wednesday 16	

Appointments **March 2022**

Tuesday 1	Thursday 17
Wednesday 2	Friday 18
Thursday 3	Saturday 19
Friday 4	**Sunday** **20**
Saturday 5	Monday 21
Sunday **6**	Tuesday 22
Monday 7	Wednesday 23
Tuesday 8	Thursday 24
Wednesday 9	Friday 25
Thursday 10	Saturday 26
Friday 11	**Sunday** **27**
Saturday 12	Monday 28
Sunday **13**	Tuesday 29
Monday 14	Wednesday 30
Tuesday 15	Thursday 31
Wednesday 16	

Appointments **April 2022**

Friday 1	Sunday **17**
Saturday 2	Monday 18
Sunday **3**	Tuesday 19
Monday 4	Wednesday 20
Tuesday 5	Thursday 21
Wednesday 6	Friday 22
Thursday 7	Saturday 23
Friday 8	**Sunday** **24**
Saturday 9	Monday 25
Sunday **10**	Tuesday 26
Monday 11	Wednesday 27
Tuesday 12	Thursday 28
Wednesday 13	Friday 29
Thursday 14	Saturday 30
Friday 15	
Saturday 16	

Appointments **May 2022**

Sunday
1

Monday
2

Tuesday
3

Wednesday
4

Thursday
5

Friday
6

Saturday
7

Sunday
8

Monday
9

Tuesday
10

Wednesday
11

Thursday
12

Friday
13

Saturday
14

Sunday
15

Monday
16

Tuesday
17

Wednesday
18

Thursday
19

Friday
20

Saturday
21

Sunday
22

Monday
23

Tuesday
24

Wednesday
25

Thursday
26

Friday
27

Saturday
28

Sunday
29

Monday
30

Tuesday
31

Appointments **June 2022**

Wednesday 1	Friday 17
Thursday 2	Saturday 18
Friday 3	**Sunday** **19**
Saturday 4	Monday 20
Sunday **5**	Tuesday 21
Monday 6	Wednesday 22
Tuesday 7	Thursday 23
Wednesday 8	Friday 24
Thursday 9	Saturday 25
Friday 10	**Sunday** **26**
Saturday 11	Monday 27
Sunday **12**	Tuesday 28
Monday 13	Wednesday 29
Tuesday 14	Thursday 30
Wednesday 15	
Thursday 16	

Haynes: the story so far

Haynes is known the world over for car and motorcycle repair manuals. It is the market leader for practical and authoritative reference works on DIY maintenance and servicing of vehicles, and has gained an enviable reputation in 60 years of publishing. Every Haynes manual is based on a complete strip-down and rebuild of a vehicle in the company's workshops, ensuring that instructions and illustrations are accurate, practical and easy to follow.

J.H. Haynes & Co. was formed on 18 May 1960, but the origins of today's publishing success can be traced back even further. In 1954, John Haynes, then aged 16 and still at school, built an Austin Seven Special and was inspired to write and publish a book on how he had done it. This was *Building a 750cc Special*, which went on sale in 1956. After leaving school, John served in the RAF but still found time to develop his long-term passion of publishing practical motoring books. The first workshop manual was published after he helped a friend restore a 'frog-eye' Austin-Healey Sprite, having found that the manufacturer's own publications were totally inadequate from a DIY point of view.

With help from his father Harold, wife Annette and younger brother David, the business was built up, always following a philosophy of self-sufficiency and direct control over all aspects of publishing. From writing, photography and editing to sales and marketing, this policy continues to the present day. As the number of employed staff increased and output expanded, various new premises were required and eventually, in 1972, the site of an old creamery on the A303 at Sparkford, near Yeovil in Somerset, was taken over – this remains the company's headquarters today.

Attention also turned to the USA and a subsidiary was set up in California in 1974. North America has since become the largest market for Haynes car repair manuals. The range of manuals available in North America was enhanced by the acquisition of former rival Chilton in 2002. Offices and subsidiary companies also operate in Australia, The Netherlands and Romania.

The continuing success of the original company led to flotation on the London Stock Exchange in 1979 and the launch of the Haynes Publishing Group PLC.

The Haynes family involvement, however, remained strong. Although he retired as Chairman upon the company's 50th anniversary, John Haynes OBE (he was recognised for his services to publishing in the Queen's 1995 Birthday Honours List) sat on the Main Board as Founder Director and remained a major shareholder until his death in 2019. His oldest son, J, who joined the business in 2002, took over as Chief Executive to steer the Group into the next phase of its evolution.

Having established a flourishing book publishing business based on his personal interest in cars and motorcycles, it was logical for John Haynes to build up a collection of vehicles that appealed to him. He started to acquire a few interesting cars in the late 1960s and the collection expanded rapidly, becoming so large that a permanent museum was required to house and maintain them all. The Haynes International Motor Museum, the Charitable Trust to which John donated almost

The very beginning. John Haynes with his 1954 Austin Seven Special, taken with a Brownie box camera.

The Haynes project workshop team hard at work on yet another manual, this time for the new Mini.

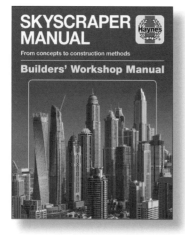

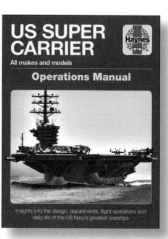

all of his collection, opened in July 1985 and, like the publishing company, subsequently grew out of all recognition. It is now the UK's largest permanent exhibition of cars and motorcycles. It is a living and working museum with more than 350 vehicles in 11 display halls together with extensive workshop facilities to ensure that exhibits are maintained in first-class operational condition.

The Haynes Group is about much more than car manuals, and more recent car and motorcycle manuals are offered through online subscription. Online Manuals and videos have been available since 2010 and provide colour imagery and video accessible through computer or tablet via an internet connection. HaynesPro offers digital solutions for the professional automotive market throughout Europe, including vehicle diagnostic data, parts information and vehicle repair information, and the acquisition of OATS Limited, a global lubricants database business based in Swindon, has provided Haynes with a presence in the oil industry while broadening the group's portfolio in the professional automotive market. In the automotive sector, the Haynes business has grown from providing DIY car manuals to providing content, data and solutions that can be delivered across a variety of platforms. In

addition to providing customers with practical information and a choice as to how they look after their vehicles, these services also facilitate competition and provide tools to increase efficiency in the professional automotive aftermarket. Meanwhile, the Haynes Practical Lifestyle division publishes an extensive range of manuals on motorsport, military, aviation, maritime and railway subjects, as well as manuals covering areas such as history, food, computing, health, sport and DIY.

In 2020 Haynes was bought by the French company Infopro Digital. Commenting on the acquisition, its Founder and Executive Chairman, Christophe Czajka, said: 'At Infopro Digital we have long respected Haynes' spirit of innovation and its reputation for excellence. With a deeply complementary product set and geographic footprint, the combined companies have an opportunity to serve our clients more effectively and to build on both organisations' history of creating innovative, transformative products that the automotive industry has come to value. We are committed to working together to create a company that will continue to help define the future of automotive data.'

To learn more and to view Haynes' entire range of publications, please visit our website **www.haynes.com.**

'If you grew up in the era when cars and motorbikes were unreliable, John Haynes was the Messiah.'
JAMES MAY

John Haynes

THE MAN BEHIND THE MANUALS
NED TEMKO

JOHN HAYNES – THE MAN BEHIND THE MANUAL
ISBN 978 178521 685 5 – £20.00
Available from www.haynes.com

Just part of the amazing 'Red Collection' of sports cars on display at the Haynes International Motor Museum.

Annette and John Haynes on the occasion of his OBE presentation.

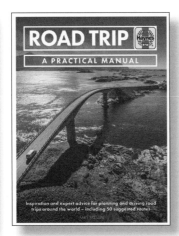

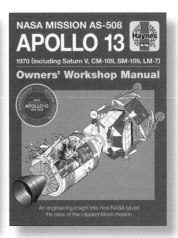

Conversion Factors

Length (distance)

Inches (in)	x 25.4	=	Millimetres (mm)	x 0.0394	=	Inches (in)
Feet (ft)	x 0.305	=	Metres (m)	x 3.281	=	Feet (ft)
Miles	x 1.609	=	Kilometres (km)	x 0.621	=	Miles

Volume (capacity)

Cubic inches (cu in; in^3)	x 16.387	=	Cubic centimetres (cc; cm^3)	x 0.061	=	Cubic inches (cu in; in^3)
Imperial pints (Imp pt)	x 0.568	=	Litres (l)	x 1.76	=	Imperial pints (Imp pt)
Imperial quarts (Imp qt)	x 1.137	=	Litres (l)	x 0.88	=	Imperial quarts (Imp qt)
Imperial quarts (Imp qt)	x 1.201	=	US quarts (US qt)	x 0.833	=	Imperial quarts (Imp qt)
US quarts (US qt)	x 0.946	=	Litres (l)	x 1.057	=	US quarts (US qt)
Imperial gallons (Imp gal)	x 4.546	=	Litres (l)	x 0.22	=	Imperial gallons (Imp gal)
Imperial gallons (Imp gal)	x 1.201	=	US gallons (US gal)	x 0.833	=	Imperial gallons (Imp gal)
US gallons (US gal)	x 3.785	=	Litres (l)	x 0.264	=	US gallons (US gal)

Mass (weight)

Ounces (oz)	x 28.35	=	Grams (g)	x 0.035	=	Ounces (oz)
Pounds (lb)	x 0.454	=	Kilograms (kg)	x 2.205	=	Pounds (lb)

Force

Ounces-force (ozf; oz)	x 0.278	=	Newtons (N)	x 3.6	=	Ounces-force (ozf; oz)
Pounds-force (lbf; lb)	x 4.448	=	Newtons (N)	x 0.225	=	Pounds-force (lbf; lb)
Newtons (N)	x 0.1	=	Kilograms-force (kgf; kg)	x 9.81	=	Newtons (N)

Pressure

Pounds-force per square inch (psi; lbf/in^2; lb/in^2)	x 0.070	=	Kilograms-force per square centimetre (kgf/cm^2; kg/cm^2)	x 14.223	=	Pounds-force per square inch (psi; lbf/in^2; lb/in^2)
Pounds-force per square inch (psi; lbf/in^2; lb/in^2)	x 0.068	=	Atmospheres (atm)	x 14.696	=	Pounds-force per square inch (psi; lbf/in^2; lb/in^2)
Pounds-force per square inch (psi; lbf/in^2; lb/in^2)	x 0.069	=	Bars	x 14.5	=	Pounds-force per square inch (psi; lbf/in^2; lb/in^2)
Pounds-force per square inch (psi; lbf/in^2; lb/in^2)	x 6.895	=	Kilopascals (kPa)	x 0.145	=	Pounds-force per square inch (psi; lbf/in^2; lb/in^2)
Kilopascals (kPa)	x 0.01	=	Kilograms-force per square centimetre (kgf/cm^2; kg/cm^2)	x 98.1	=	Kilopascals (kPa)
Millibar (mbar)	x 100	=	Pascals (Pa)	x 0.01	=	Millibar (mbar)
Millibar (mbar)	x 0.0145	=	Pounds-force per square inch (psi; lbf/in^2; lb/in^2)	x 68.947	=	Millibar (mbar)
Millibar (mbar)	x 0.75	=	Millimetres of mercury (mmHg)	x 1.333	=	Millibar (mbar)
Millibar (mbar)	x 0.401	=	Inches of water (inH$_2$O)	x 2.491	=	Millibar (mbar)
Millimetres of mercury (mmHg)	x 0.535	=	Inches of water (inH$_2$O)	x 1.868	=	Millimetres of mercury (mmHg)
Inches of water (inH$_2$O)	x 0.036	=	Pounds-force per square inch (psi; lbf/in^2; lb/in^2)	x 27.68	=	Inches of water (inH$_2$O)

Torque (moment of force)

Pounds-force inches (lbf in; lb in)	x 1.152	=	Kilograms-force centimetre (kgf cm; kg cm)	x 0.868	=	Pounds-force inches (lbf in; lb in)
Pounds-force inches (lbf in; lb in)	x 0.113	=	Newton metres (Nm)	x 8.85	=	Pounds-force inches (lbf in; lb in)
Pounds-force inches (lbf in; lb in)	x 0.083	=	Pounds-force feet (lbf ft; lb ft)	x 12	=	Pounds-force inches (lbf in; lb in)
Pounds-force feet (lbf ft; lb ft)	x 0.138	=	Kilograms-force metres (kgf m; kg m)	x 7.233	=	Pounds-force feet (lbf ft; lb ft)
Pounds-force feet (lbf ft; lb ft)	x 1.356	=	Newton metres (Nm)	x 0.738	=	Pounds-force feet (lbf ft; lb ft)
Newton metres (Nm)	x 0.102	=	Kilograms-force metres (kgf m; kg m)	x 9.804	=	Newton metres (Nm)

Power

Horsepower (hp)	x 745.7	=	Watts (W)	x 0.0013	=	Horsepower (hp)

Velocity (speed)

Miles per hour (miles/hr; mph)	x 1.609	=	Kilometres per hour (km/hr; kph)	x 0.621	=	Miles per hour (miles/hr; mph)

Fuel consumption*

Miles per gallon, Imperial (mpg)	x 0.354	=	Kilometres per litre (km/l)	x 2.825	=	Miles per gallon, Imperial (mpg)
Miles per gallon, US (mpg)	x 0.425	=	Kilometres per litre (km/l)	x 2.352	=	Miles per gallon, US (mpg)

Temperature

Degrees Fahrenheit = (°C x 1.8) + 32   Degrees Celsius (Degrees Centigrade; °C) = (°F − 32) x 0.56

It is common practice to convert from miles per gallon (mpg) to litres/100 kilometres (l/100km), where mpg x l/100 km = 282

UK MAINLAND VEHICLE
REGISTRATION LETTERS

Registration marks:

From 1 September 2001 registration marks took the form:
AB52 CCC where **A** is the area identifier, **B** is the vehicle
registration office. **52** identifies the year, the first digit is the
period, either **0** or **1** (March to August) or **5** or **6** (September
to February), the second digit is the year in which the period
starts. **CCC** is a random combination of letters.

The registration letter should not be regarded as an infallible
indication of vehicle age. **Refer to the registration document
for confirmation.**

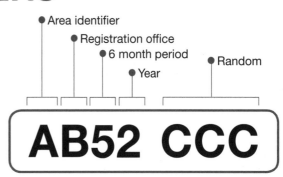

● Area identifier
● Registration office
● 6 month period
● Year
● Random

AB52 CCC

SUFFIX				
Jan 1 1963	>	Dec 31 1963		**A**
Jan 1 1964	>	Dec 31 1964		**B**
Jan 1 1965	>	Dec 31 1965		**C**
Jan 1 1966	>	Dec 31 1966		**D**
Jan 1 1967	>	July 31 1967		**E**
Aug 1 1967	>	July 31 1968		**F**
Aug 1 1968	>	July 31 1969		**G**
Aug 1 1969	>	July 31 1970		**H**
Aug 1 1970	>	July 31 1971		**J**
Aug 1 1971	>	July 31 1972		**K**
Aug 1 1972	>	July 31 1973		**L**
Aug 1 1973	>	July 31 1974		**M**
Aug 1 1974	>	July 31 1975		**N**
Aug 1 1975	>	July 31 1976		**P**
Aug 1 1976	>	July 31 1977		**R**
Aug 1 1977	>	July 31 1978		**S**
Aug 1 1978	>	July 31 1979		**T**
Aug 1 1979	>	July 31 1980		**V**
Aug 1 1980	>	July 31 1981		**W**
Aug 1 1981	>	July 31 1982		**X**
Aug 1 1982	>	July 31 1983		**Y**

PREFIX				
A	Aug 1 1983	>	July 31 1984	
B	Aug 1 1984	>	July 31 1985	
C	Aug 1 1985	>	July 31 1986	
D	Aug 1 1986	>	July 31 1987	
E	Aug 1 1987	>	July 31 1988	
F	Aug 1 1988	>	July 31 1989	
G	Aug 1 1989	>	July 31 1990	
H	Aug 1 1990	>	July 31 1991	
J	Aug 1 1991	>	July 31 1992	
K	Aug 1 1992	>	July 31 1993	
L	Aug 1 1993	>	July 31 1994	
M	Aug 1 1994	>	July 31 1995	
N	Aug 1 1995	>	July 31 1996	
P	Aug 1 1996	>	July 31 1997	
R	Aug 1 1997	>	July 31 1998	
S	Aug 1 1998	>	Jan 31 1999	
T	Feb 1 1999	>	July 31 1999	
V	Aug 1 1999	>	Feb 29 2000	
W	Mar 1 2000	>	Aug 31 2000	
X	Sept 1 2000	>	Feb 28 2001	
Y	Mar 1 2001	>	Aug 31 2001	

CENTRAL				
Sept 1 2001	>	Feb 28 2002	**51**
Mar 1 2002	>	Aug 31 2002	**02**
Sept 1 2002	>	Feb 28 2003	**52**
Mar 1 2003	>	Aug 31 2003	**03**
Sept 1 2003	>	Feb 29 2004	**53**
Mar 1 2004	>	Aug 31 2004	**04**
Sept 1 2004	>	Feb 28 2005	**54**
Mar 1 2005	>	Aug 31 2005	**05**
Sept 1 2005	>	Feb 28 2006	**55**
Mar 1 2006	>	Aug 31 2006	**06**
Sept 1 2006	>	Feb 28 2007	**56**
Mar 1 2007	>	Aug 31 2007	**07**
Sept 1 2007	>	Feb 29 2008	**57**
Mar 1 2008	>	Aug 31 2008	**08**
Sept 1 2008	>	Feb 28 2009	**58**
Mar 1 2009	>	Aug 31 2009	**09**
Sept 1 2009	>	Feb 28 2010	**59**
Mar 1 2010	>	Aug 31 2010	**10**
Sept 1 2010	>	Feb 28 2011	**60**
Mar 1 2011	>	Aug 31 2011	**11**
Sept 1 2011	>	Feb 29 2012	**61**
Mar 1 2012	>	Aug 31 2012	**12**
Sept 1 2012	>	Feb 28 2013	**62**
Mar 1 2013	>	Aug 31 2013	**13**
Sept 1 2013	>	Feb 28 2014	**63**
Mar 1 2014	>	Aug 31 2014	**14**
Sept 1 2014	>	Feb 28 2015	**64**
Mar 1 2015	>	Aug 31 2015	**15**
Sept 1 2015	>	Feb 29 2016	**65**
Mar 1 2016	>	Aug 31 2016	**16**
Sept 1 2016	>	Feb 28 2017	**66**
Mar 1 2017	>	Aug 31 2017	**17**
Sept 1 2017	>	Feb 28 2018	**67**
Mar 1 2018	>	Aug 31 2018	**18**
Sept 1 2018	>	Feb 28 2019	**68**
Mar 1 2019	>	Aug 31 2019	**19**
Sept 1 2019	>	Feb 28 2020	**69**
Mar 1 2020	>	Aug 31 2020	**20**
Sept 1 2020	>	Feb 29 2021	**70**
Mar 1 2021	>	Aug 31 2021	**21**
Sept 1 2021	>	Feb 28 2022	**71**

On the next four pages you will find a complete list of **registration area
identification letters** covering the three periods: **pre-1974**, **1974 to 2001** and
September 2001 onwards.

UK Number Plate Registration Area Identification Letters

	Pre-1974	1974 to 2001	September 2001 onwards
A	London	–	–
AA	Hampshire	Bournemouth	Peterborough
AB	Worcestershire	Worcester	Peterborough
AC	Warwickshire	Coventry	Peterborough
AD	Gloucestershire	Gloucester	Peterborough
AE	Bristol	Bristol	Peterborough
AF	Cornwall	Truro	Peterborough
AG	Ayrshire	Kingston upon Hull	Peterborough
AH	Norfolk	Norwich	Peterborough
AI	Meath	–	–
AJ	North Yorkshire	Middlesbrough	Peterborough
AK	Bradford	Sheffield	Peterborough
AL	Nottinghamshire	Nottingham	Peterborough
AM	Wiltshire	Swindon	Peterborough
AN	West Ham	Reading	Peterborough
AO	Cumberland	Carlisle	Norwich
AP	East Sussex	Brighton	Norwich
AR	Hertfordshire	Chelmsford	Norwich
AS	Nairn	Inverness	Norwich
AT	Kingston upon Hull	Kingston upon Hull	Norwich
AU	Nottingham	Nottingham	Norwich
AV	Aberdeenshire	Peterborough	Ipswich
AW	Shropshire	Shrewsbury	Ipswich
AX	Monmouthshire	Cardiff	Ipswich
AY	Leicestershire	Leicester	Ipswich
AY	Alderney	Alderney	Ipswich
AZ	Belfast	Belfast	–
B	Lancashire	–	–
BA	Salford	Manchester	Birmingham
BB	Newcastle upon Tyne	Newcastle upon Tyne	Birmingham
BC	Leicester	Leicester	Birmingham
BD	Northamptonshire	Northampton	Birmingham
BE	Lincolnshire	Lincoln	Birmingham
BF	Staffordshire	Stoke-on-Trent	Birmingham
BG	Birkenhead	Liverpool	Birmingham
BH	Buckinghamshire	Luton	Birmingham
BI	Monaghan	–	Birmingham
BJ	East Suffolk	Ipswich	Birmingham
BK	Portsmouth	Portsmouth	Birmingham
BL	Berkshire	Reading	Birmingham
BM	Bedfordshire	Luton	Birmingham
BN	Bolton	Manchester	Birmingham
BO	Cardiff	Cardiff	Birmingham
BP	West Sussex	Portsmouth	Birmingham
BR	Sunderland	Newcastle upon Tyne	Birmingham
BS	Orkney	Aberdeen	Birmingham
BT	East Yorkshire	Leeds	Birmingham
BU	Oldham	Manchester	Birmingham
BV	Blackburn	Preston	Birmingham
BW	Oxfordshire	Oxford	Birmingham
BX	Carmarthenshire	Haverfordwest	Birmingham
BY	Croydon	North West London	Birmingham
BZ	Down	Belfast	–
C	West Yorkshire	–	–
CA	Denbighshire	Chester	Cardiff
CB	Blackburn	Manchester	Cardiff
CC	Caernarvonshire	Bangor	Cardiff
CD	Brighton	Brighton	Cardiff
CE	Cambridgeshire	Peterborough	Cardiff
CF	West Suffolk	Reading	Cardiff
CG	Hampshire	Bournemouth	Cardiff
CH	Derby	Nottingham	Cardiff
CI	Laois	–	–
CJ	Herefordshire	Gloucester	Cardiff
CK	Preston	Preston	Cardiff
CL	Norwich	Norwich	Cardiff
CM	Birkenhead	Liverpool	Cardiff
CN	Gateshead	Newcastle upon Tyne	Cardiff
CO	Plymouth	Exeter	Cardiff
CP	Halifax	Huddersfield	Swansea
CR	Southampton	Portsmouth	Swansea
CS	Ayrshire	Glasgow	Swansea
CT	Lincolnshire	Lincoln	Swansea
CU	South Shields	Newcastle upon Tyne	Swansea
CV	Cornwall	Truro	Swansea
CW	Burnley	Preston	Bangor
CX	Huddersfield	Huddersfield	Bangor
CY	Swansea	Swansea	Bangor
CZ	Belfast	–	–

	Pre-1974	1974 to 2001	September 2001 onwards
D	Kent	–	–
DA	Wolverhampton	Birmingham	Chester
DB	Stockport	Manchester	Chester
DC	Middlesbrough	Middlesbrough	Chester
DD	Gloucestershire	Gloucester	Chester
DE	Pembrokeshire	Haverfordwest	Chester
DF	Gloucestershire	Gloucester	Chester
DG	Gloucestershire	Gloucester	Chester
DH	Walsall	Dudley	Chester
DI	Roscommon	–	–
DJ	St Helens	Liverpool	Chester
DK	Rochdale	Manchester	Chester
DL	Isle of Wight	Portsmouth	Shrewsbury
DM	Flintshire	Chester	Shrewsbury
DN	York	Leeds	Shrewsbury
DO	Lincolnshire	Lincoln	Shrewsbury
DP	Reading	Reading	Shrewsbury
DR	Plymouth	Exeter	Shrewsbury
DS	Peeblesshire	Glasgow	Shrewsbury
DT	Doncaster	Sheffield	Shrewsbury
DU	Coventry	Coventry	Shrewsbury
DV	Devon	Exeter	Shrewsbury
DW	Newport	Cardiff	Shrewsbury
DX	Ipswich	Ipswich	Shrewsbury
DY	Hastings	Brighton	Shrewsbury
DZ	Antrim	Belfast	–
E	Staffordshire	–	–
EA	West Bromwich	Dudley	Chelmsford
EB	Isle of Ely	Peterborough	Chelmsford
EC	Westmorland	Preston	Chelmsford
ED	Warrington	Liverpool	Chelmsford
EE	Grimsby	Lincoln	Chelmsford
EF	West Hartlepool	Middlesbrough	Chelmsford
EG	Peterborough	Peterborough	Chelmsford
EH	Stoke-on-Trent	Stoke-on-Trent	Chelmsford
EI	Sligo	–	–
EJ	Cardigan	Haverfordwest	Chelmsford
EK	Wigan	Liverpool	Chelmsford
EL	Bournemouth	Bournemouth	Chelmsford
EM	Bootle	Liverpool	Chelmsford
EN	Bury	Manchester	Chelmsford
EO	Barrow-in-Furness	Preston	Chelmsford
EP	Montgomery	Swansea	Chelmsford
ER	Cambridgeshire	Peterborough	Chelmsford
ES	Perthshire	Dundee	Chelmsford
ET	Rotherham	Sheffield	Chelmsford
EU	Brecknockshire	Bristol	Chelmsford
EV	Essex	Chelmsford	Chelmsford
EW	Huntingdon	Peterborough	Chelmsford
EX	Great Yarmouth	Norwich	Chelmsford
EY	Anglesey	Bangor	Chelmsford
EZ	Belfast	–	–
FA	Burton on Trent	Stoke-on-Trent	Nottingham
FB	Bath	Bristol	Nottingham
FC	Oxford	Oxford	Nottingham
FD	Dudley	Dudley	Nottingham
FE	Lincoln	Lincoln	Nottingham
FF	Merioneth	Bangor	Nottingham
FG	Fife	Brighton	Nottingham
FH	Gloucester	Gloucester	Nottingham
FI	Tipperary	–	–
FJ	Exeter	Exeter	Nottingham
FK	Worcester	Dudley	Nottingham
FL	Peterborough	Peterborough	Nottingham
FM	Chester	Chester	Nottingham
FN	Canterbury	Maidstone	Nottingham
FO	Radnorshire	Gloucester	Nottingham
FP	Rutland	Leicester	Nottingham
FR	Blackpool	Preston	Lincoln
FS	Edinburgh	Edinburgh	Lincoln
FT	Tynemouth	Newcastle upon Tyne	Lincoln
FU	Lincolnshire	Lincoln	Lincoln
FV	Blackpool	Preston	Lincoln
FW	Lincolnshire	Lincoln	Lincoln
FX	Dorset	Bournemouth	Lincoln
FY	Southport	Liverpool	Lincoln
FZ	Belfast	–	–
G	Glasgow		
GA	Glasgow	Glasgow	Maidstone

	Pre-1974	1974 to 2001	September 2001 onwards
GB	Glasgow	Glasgow	Maidstone
GC	London	South West London	Maidstone
GD	Glasgow	Glasgow	Maidstone
GE	Glasgow	Glasgow	Maidstone
GF	London	South West London	Maidstone
GG	Glasgow	Glasgow	Maidstone
GH	London	South West London	Maidstone
GJ	London	South West London	Maidstone
GK	London	South West London	Maidstone
GL	Bath	Truro	Maidstone
GM	Motherwell	Reading	Maidstone
GN	London	South West London	Maidstone
GO	London	South West London	Maidstone
GP	London	South West London	Brighton
GR	Sunderland	Newcastle upon Tyne	Brighton
GS	Perthshire	Luton	Brighton
GT	London	South West London	Brighton
GU	London	South East London	Brighton
GV	West Suffolk	Ipswich	Brighton
GW	London	South East London	Brighton
GX	London	South East London	Brighton
GY	London	South East London	Brighton
GZ	Belfast	–	–
H	Middlesex	–	–
HA	Smethwick	Dudley	Bournemouth
HB	Merthyr Tydfil	Cardiff	Bournemouth
HC	Eastbourne	Brighton	Bournemouth
HD	Dewsbury	Huddersfield	Bournemouth
HE	Barnsley	Sheffield	Bournemouth
HF	Wallasey	Liverpool	Bournemouth
HG	Burnley	Preston	Bournemouth
HH	Carlisle	Carlisle	Bournemouth
HI	Tipperary	–	–
HJ	Southend	Chelmsford	Bournemouth
HK	Essex	Chelmsford	Portsmouth
HL	Wakefield	Sheffield	Portsmouth
HM	East Ham	Central London	Portsmouth
HN	Darlington	Middlesbrough	Portsmouth
HO	Hampshire	Bournemouth	Portsmouth
HP	Coventry	Coventry	Portsmouth
HR	Wiltshire	Swindon	Portsmouth
HS	Renfrewshire	Glasgow	Portsmouth
HT	Bristol	Bristol	Portsmouth
HU	Bristol	Bristol	Portsmouth
HV	East Ham	Central London	Portsmouth
HW	Bristol	Bristol	Isle of Wight
HX	Middlesex	Central London	Portsmouth
HY	Bristol	Bristol	Portsmouth
HZ	Tyrone	–	–
IA	Antrim	Belfast	–
IB	Armagh	Belfast	–
IC	Carlow	–	–
ID	Cavan	–	–
IE	Clare	–	–
IF	Cork	–	–
IH	Donegal	–	–
IJ	Down	Belfast	–
IK	Dublin	–	–
IL	Fermanagh	Belfast	–
IM	Galway	–	–
IN	Kerry	–	–
IO	Kildare	–	–
IP	Kilkenny	–	–
IR	Offaly	–	–
IT	Leitrim	–	–
IU	Limerick	–	–
IW	Londonderry	Belfast	–
IX	Longford	–	–
IY	Louth	–	–
IZ	Mayo	–	–
J	Durham	–	–
J	Jersey	Jersey	–
JA	Stockport	Manchester	–
JB	Berkshire	Reading	–
JC	Caernarvonshire	Bangor	–
JD	West Ham	Central London	–
JE	Isle of Ely	Peterborough	–
JF	Leicester	Leicester	–
JG	Canterbury	Maidstone	–
JH	Hertfordshire	Reading	–
JI	Tyrone	Belfast	–
JJ	London	Maidstone	

	Pre-1974	1974 to 2001	September 2001 onwards
JK	Eastbourne	Brighton	–
JL	Lincolnshire	Lincoln	–
JM	Westmorland	Reading	–
JN	Southend	Chelmsford	–
JO	Oxford	Oxford	–
JP	Wigan	Liverpool	–
JR	Northumberland	Newcastle upon Tyne	–
JS	Ross and Cromarty	Inverness	–
JT	Dorset	Bournemouth	–
JU	Leicestershire	Leicester	–
JV	Grimsby	Lincoln	–
JW	Wolverhampton	Birmingham	–
JX	Halifax	Huddersfield	–
JY	Plymouth	Exeter	–
JZ	Down	–	–
K	Liverpool	–	–
KA	Liverpool	Liverpool	Luton
KB	Liverpool	Liverpool	Luton
KC	Liverpool	Liverpool	Luton
KD	Liverpool	Liverpool	Luton
KE	Kent	Maidstone	Luton
KF	Liverpool	Liverpool	Luton
KG	Cardiff	Cardiff	Luton
KH	Kingston upon Hull	Kingston upon Hull	Luton
KI	Waterford	–	–
KJ	Kent	Maidstone	Luton
KK	Kent	Maidstone	Luton
KL	Kent	Maidstone	Luton
KM	Kent	Maidstone	Northampton
KN	Kent	Maidstone	Northampton
KO	Kent	Maidstone	Northampton
KP	Kent	Maidstone	Northampton
KR	Kent	Maidstone	Northampton
KS	Roxburghshire	Edinburgh	Northampton
KT	Kent	Maidstone	Northampton
KU	Bradford	Sheffield	Northampton
KV	Coventry	Coventry	Northampton
KW	Bradford	Sheffield	Northampton
KX	Buckinghamshire	Luton	Northampton
KY	Bradford	Sheffield	Northampton
KZ	Antrim	–	–
L	Glamorgan	–	–
LA	London	North West London	Wimbledon
LB	London	North West London	Wimbledon
LC	London	North West London	Wimbledon
LD	London	North West London	Wimbledon
LE	London	North West London	Wimbledon
LF	London	North West London	Wimbledon
LG	Cheshire	Chester	Wimbledon
LH	London	North West London	Wimbledon
LI	Westmeath	–	–
LJ	Bournemouth	Bournemouth	Wimbledon
LK	London	North West London	Stanmore
LL	London	North West London	Stanmore
LM	London	North West London	Stanmore
LN	London	North West London	Stanmore
LO	London	North West London	Stanmore
LP	London	North West London	Stanmore
LR	London	North West London	Stanmore
LS	Selkirk	Edinburgh	Stanmore
LT	London	North West London	Stanmore
LU	London	North West London	Sidcup
LV	Liverpool	Liverpool	Sidcup
LW	London	North West London	Sidcup
LX	London	North West London	Sidcup
LY	London	North West London	Sidcup
LZ	Armagh	–	–
M	Cheshire	–	–
MA	Cheshire	Chester	Manchester
MAN	Isle of Man	Isle of Man	–
MB	Cheshire	Chester	Manchester
MC	Middlesex	North East London	Manchester
MD	Middlesex	North East London	Manchester
ME	Middlesex	North East London	Manchester
MF	Middlesex	North East London	Manchester
MG	Middlesex	North East London	Manchester
MH	Middlesex	North East London	Manchester
MI	Wexford	–	–
MJ	Bedfordshire	Luton	Manchester
MK	Middlesex	North East London	Manchester
ML	Middlesex	North East London	Manchester
MM	Middlesex	North East London	Manchester

	Pre-1974	1974 to 2001	September 2001 onwards
MN	Isle of Man	Isle of Man	Isle of Man
MO	Berkshire	Reading	Manchester
MP	Middlesex	North East London	Manchester
MR	Wiltshire	Swindon	Manchester
MS	Stirlingshire	Edinburgh	Manchester
MT	Middlesex	North East London	Manchester
MU	Middlesex	North East London	Manchester
MV	Middlesex	South East London	Manchester
MW	Wiltshire	Swindon	Manchester
MX	Middlesex	South East London	Manchester
MY	Middlesex	South East London	Manchester
MZ	Belfast	–	–
N	Manchester	–	–
NA	Manchester	Manchester	Newcastle upon Tyne
NB	Manchester	Manchester	Newcastle upon Tyne
NC	Manchester	Manchester	Newcastle upon Tyne
ND	Manchester	Manchester	Newcastle upon Tyne
NE	Manchester	Manchester	Newcastle upon Tyne
NF	Manchester	Manchester	Newcastle upon Tyne
NG	Norfolk	Norwich	Newcastle upon Tyne
NH	Northampton	Northampton	Newcastle upon Tyne
NI	Wicklow	–	–
NJ	East Sussex	Brighton	Newcastle upon Tyne
NK	Hertfordshire	Luton	Newcastle upon Tyne
NL	Northumberland	Newcastle upon Tyne	Newcastle upon Tyne
NM	Bedfordshire	Luton	Newcastle upon Tyne
NN	Nottinghamshire	Nottingham	Newcastle upon Tyne
NO	Essex	Chelmsford	Newcastle upon Tyne
NP	Worcestershire	Worcester	Stockton-on-Tees
NR	Leicestershire	Leicester	Stockton-on-Tees
NS	Sutherland	Glasgow	Stockton-on-Tees
NT	Shropshire	Shrewsbury	Stockton-on-Tees
NU	Derbyshire	Nottingham	Stockton-on-Tees
NV	Northamptonshire	Northampton	Stockton-on-Tees
NW	Leeds	Leeds	Stockton-on-Tees
NX	Warwickshire	Dudley	Stockton-on-Tees
NY	Glamorgan	Cardiff	Stockton-on-Tees
NZ	Londonderry	–	–
O	Birmingham	–	–
OA	Birmingham	Birmingham	Oxford
OB	Birmingham	Birmingham	Oxford
OC	Birmingham	Birmingham	Oxford
OD	Devon	Exeter	Oxford
OE	Birmingham	Birmingham	Oxford
OF	Birmingham	Birmingham	Oxford
OG	Birmingham	Birmingham	Oxford
OH	Birmingham	Birmingham	Oxford
OI	Belfast	Belfast	–
OJ	Birmingham	Birmingham	Oxford
OK	Birmingham	Birmingham	Oxford
OL	Birmingham	Birmingham	Oxford
OM	Birmingham	Birmingham	Oxford
ON	Birmingham	Birmingham	Oxford
OO	Essex	Chelmsford	Oxford
OP	Birmingham	Birmingham	Oxford
OR	Hampshire	Portsmouth	Oxford
OS	Wigtownshire	Glasgow	Oxford
OT	Hampshire	Portsmouth	Oxford
OU	Hampshire	Bristol	Oxford
OV	Birmingham	Birmingham	Oxford
OW	Southampton	Portsmouth	Oxford
OX	Birmingham	Birmingham	Oxford
OY	Croydon	North West London	Oxford
OZ	Belfast	–	–
P	Surrey	–	–
PA	Surrey	Guildford	Preston
PB	Surrey	Guildford	Preston
PC	Surrey	Guildford	Preston
PD	Surrey	Guildford	Preston
PE	Surrey	Guildford	Preston
PF	Surrey	Guildford	Preston
PG	Surrey	Guildford	Preston
PH	Surrey	Guildford	Preston
PI	Cork	–	–
PJ	Surrey	Guildford	Preston
PK	Surrey	Guildford	Preston
PL	Surrey	Guildford	Preston
PM	East Sussex	Guildford	Preston
PN	East Sussex	Brighton	Preston
PO	West Sussex	Portsmouth	Preston
PP	Buckinghamshire	Luton	Preston
PR	Dorset	Bournemouth	Preston

	Pre-1974	1974 to 2001	September 2001 onwards
PS	Shetland	Aberdeen	Preston
PT	Durham	Newcastle upon Tyne	Preston
PU	Essex	Chelmsford	Carlisle
PV	Ipswich	Ipswich	Carlisle
PW	Norfolk	Norwich	Carlisle
PX	West Sussex	Portsmouth	Carlisle
PY	North Yorkshire	Middlesbrough	Carlisle
PZ	Belfast	–	–
R	Derbyshire	–	–
RA	Derbyshire	Nottingham	Reading
RB	Derbyshire	Nottingham	Reading
RC	Derby	Nottingham	Reading
RD	Reading	Reading	Reading
RE	Staffordshire	Stoke-on-Trent	Reading
RF	Staffordshire	Stoke-on-Trent	Reading
RG	Aberdeen	Newcastle upon Tyne	Reading
RH	Kingston upon Hull	Kingston upon Hull	Reading
RI	Dublin	–	–
RJ	Salford	Manchester	Reading
RK	Croydon	North West London	Reading
RL	Cornwall	Truro	Reading
RM	Cumberland	Carlisle	Reading
RN	Preston	Preston	Reading
RO	Hertfordshire	Luton	Reading
RP	Northamptonshire	Northampton	Reading
RR	Nottinghamshire	Nottingham	Reading
RS	Aberdeen	Aberdeen	Reading
RT	East Suffolk	Ipswich	Reading
RU	Bournemouth	Bournemouth	Reading
RV	Portsmouth	Portsmouth	Reading
RW	Coventry	Coventry	Reading
RX	Berkshire	Reading	Reading
RY	Leicester	Leicester	Reading
RZ	Antrim	–	–
S	Edinburgh	–	–
SA	Aberdeen	Aberdeen	Glasgow
SB	Argyllshire	Glasgow	Glasgow
SC	Edinburgh	Edinburgh	Glasgow
SD	Ayrshire	Glasgow	Glasgow
SE	Banffshire	Aberdeen	Glasgow
SF	Edinburgh	Edinburgh	Glasgow
SG	Edinburgh	Edinburgh	Glasgow
SH	Berwickshire	Edinburgh	Glasgow
SJ	Bute	Glasgow	Glasgow
SK	Caithness	Inverness	Edinburgh
SL	Clackmannanshire	Dundee	Edinburgh
SM	Dumfries	Carlisle	Edinburgh
SN	Dunbarton	Dundee	Edinburgh
SO	Morayshire	Aberdeen	Edinburgh
SP	Fifeshire	Dundee	Dundee
SR	Angus	Dundee	Dundee
SS	East Lothian	Aberdeen	Dundee
ST	Inverness	Inverness	Dundee
SU	Kincardine	Glasgow	Aberdeen
SV	Kinross	–	Aberdeen
SW	Kirkcudbright	Carlisle	Aberdeen
SX	West Lothian	Edinburgh	Inverness
SY	Midlothian	–	Inverness
SZ	Down	–	–
T	Devon	–	–
TA	Devon	Exeter	–
TB	Lancashire	Liverpool	–
TC	Lancashire	Bristol	–
TD	Lancashire	Manchester	–
TE	Lancashire	Manchester	–
TF	Lancashire	Reading	–
TG	Glamorgan	Cardiff	–
TH	Carmarthen	Swansea	–
TI	Limerick	–	–
TJ	Lancashire	Liverpool	–
TK	Dorset	Exeter	–
TL	Lincolnshire	Lincoln	–
TM	Bedfordshire	Luton	–
TN	Newcastle upon Tyne	Newcastle upon Tyne	–
TO	Nottingham	Nottingham	–
TP	Portsmouth	Portsmouth	–
TR	Southampton	Portsmouth	–
TS	Dundee	Dundee	–
TT	Devon	Exeter	–
TU	Cheshire	Chester	–
TV	Nottingham	Nottingham	–
TW	Essex	Chelmsford	–

	Pre-1974	1974 to 2001	September 2001 onwards
TX	Glamorgan	Cardiff	–
TY	Northumberland	Newcastle upon Tyne	–
TZ	Belfast	–	–
U	Leeds	–	–
UA	Leeds	Leeds	–
UB	Leeds	Leeds	–
UC	London	Central London	–
UD	Oxfordshire	Oxford	–
UE	Warwickshire	Dudley	–
UF	Brighton	Brighton	–
UG	Leeds	Leeds	–
UH	Cardiff	Cardiff	–
UI	Londonderry	Belfast	–
UJ	Shropshire	Shrewsbury	–
UK	Wolverhampton	Birmingham	–
UL	London	Central London	–
UM	Leeds	Leeds	–
UN	Denbighshire	Exeter	–
UO	Devon	Exeter	–
UP	Durham	Newcastle upon Tyne	–
UR	Hertfordshire	Luton	–
US	Glasgow	Glasgow	–
UT	Leicestershire	Leicester	–
UU	London	Central London	–
UV	London	Central London	–
UW	London	Central London	–
UX	Shropshire	Shrewsbury	–
UY	Worcestershire	Worcester	–
UZ	Belfast	–	–
V	Lanarkshire	–	–
VA	Lanarkshire	Peterborough	Worcester
VB	Croydon	Maidstone	Worcester
VC	Coventry	Coventry	Worcester
VD	Lanarkshire	–	Worcester
VE	Cambridgeshire	Peterborough	Worcester
VF	Norfolk	Norwich	Worcester
VG	Norwich	Norwich	Worcester
VH	Huddersfield	Huddersfield	Worcester
VJ	Herefordshire	Gloucester	Worcester
VK	Newcastle upon Tyne	Newcastle upon Tyne	Worcester
VL	Lincoln	Lincoln	Worcester
VM	Manchester	Manchester	Worcester
VN	North Yorkshire	Middlesbrough	Worcester
VO	Nottinghamshire	Nottingham	Worcester
VP	Birmingham	Birmingham	Worcester
VR	Manchester	Manchester	Worcester
VS	Greenock	Luton	Worcester
VT	Stoke-on-Trent	Stoke-on-Trent	Worcester
VU	Manchester	Manchester	Worcester
VV	Northampton	Northampton	Worcester
VW	Essex	Chelmsford	Worcester
VX	Essex	Chelmsford	Worcester
VY	York	Leeds	Worcester
VZ	Tyrone	–	–
W	Sheffield	–	–
WA	Sheffield	Sheffield	Exeter
WB	Sheffield	Sheffield	Exeter
WC	Essex	Chelmsford	Exeter
WD	Warwickshire	Dudley	Exeter
WE	Sheffield	Sheffield	Exeter
WF	East Yorkshire	Sheffield	Exeter
WG	Stirlingshire	Sheffield	Exeter
WH	Bolton	Manchester	Exeter
WI	Waterford	–	–
WJ	Sheffield	Sheffield	Exeter
WK	Coventry	Coventry	Truro
WL	Oxford	Oxford	Truro
WM	Southport	Liverpool	Bristol
WN	Swansea	Swansea	Bristol
WO	Monmouthshire	Cardiff	Bristol
WP	Worcestershire	Worcester	Bristol
WR	West Yorkshire	Leeds	Bristol
WS	Edinburgh	Bristol	Bristol
WT	West Yorkshire	Leeds	Bristol
WU	West Yorkshire	Leeds	Bristol
WV	Wiltshire	Brighton	Bristol
WW	West Yorkshire	Leeds	Bristol
WX	West Yorkshire	Leeds	Bristol
WY	West Yorkshire	Leeds	Bristol
WZ	Belfast	–	–
X	Northumberland	–	–
XA	London	–	–
XB	London	–	–
XC	London	–	–
XD	London	–	–
XE	London	–	–
XF	London	–	–
XG	Middlesbrough	–	–
XH	London	–	–
XI	Belfast	Belfast	–
XJ	Manchester	–	–
XK	London	–	–
XL	London	–	–
XM	London	–	–
XN	London	–	–
XO	London	–	–
XP	London	–	–
XR	London	–	–
XS	Paisley	–	–
XT	London	–	–
XU	London	–	–
XV	London	–	–
XW	London	–	–
XX	London	–	–
XY	London	–	–
XZ	Armagh	–	–
Y	Somerset	–	–
YA	Somerset	Taunton	Leeds
YB	Somerset	Taunton	Leeds
YC	Somerset	Taunton	Leeds
YD	Somerset	Taunton	Leeds
YE	London	Central London	Leeds
YF	London	Central London	Leeds
YG	West Yorkshire	Leeds	Leeds
YH	London	Central London	Leeds
YI	Dublin	–	–
YJ	Dundee	Brighton	Leeds
YK	London	Central London	Leeds
YL	London	Central London	Sheffield
YM	London	Central London	Sheffield
YN	London	Central London	Sheffield
YO	London	Central London	Sheffield
YP	London	Central London	Sheffield
YR	London	Central London	Sheffield
YS	Glasgow	Glasgow	Sheffield
YT	London	Central London	Sheffield
YU	London	Central London	Sheffield
YV	London	Central London	Beverley
YW	London	Central London	Beverley
YX	London	Central London	Beverley
YY	London	Central London	Beverley
YZ	Londonderry	–	–
Z	Dublin	–	–
ZA	Dublin	–	–
ZB	Cork	–	–
ZC	Dublin	–	–
ZD	Dublin	–	–
ZE	Dublin	–	–
ZF	Cork	–	–
ZH	Dublin	–	–
ZI	Dublin	–	–
ZJ	Dublin	–	–
ZK	Cork	–	–
ZL	Dublin	–	–
ZM	Galway	–	–
ZN	Meath	–	–
ZO	Dublin	–	–
ZP	Donegal	–	–
ZR	Wexford	–	–
ZT	Cork	–	–
ZU	Dublin	–	–
ZW	Kildare	–	–
ZX	Kerry	–	–
ZY	Louth	–	–
ZZ	Dublin	–	–

UK Distance Table

	LONDON	Aberdeen	Aberystwyth	Birmingham	Bournemouth	Brighton	Bristol	Cambridge	Cardiff	Carlisle	Chester	Derby	Dover	Edinburgh	Exeter	Fishguard	Fort William	Glasgow	Harwich	Holyhead
LONDON		806	341	179	169	89	183	84	249	484	298	198	117	608	275	422	818	634	114	420
Aberdeen	501		724	658	903	895	789	742	792	349	571	634	924	198	911	795	254	241	848	692
Aberystwyth	212	450		193	328	425	206	354	177	375	153	222	459	526	325	90	708	525	460	182
Birmingham	111	409	120		237	267	132	161	163	309	117	63	296	460	259	283	642	459	267	246
Bournemouth	105	561	204	147		148	124	251	195	554	351	306	278	705	132	375	887	703	283	463
Brighton	55	556	264	166	92		217	180	288	573	386	286	130	697	275	468	906	723	203	509
Bristol	114	490	128	82	77	135		233	71	439	237	195	314	591	121	251	722	589	314	340
Cambridge	52	461	220	100	156	112	145		290	417	269	155	204	544	351	436	750	566	106	391
Cardiff	155	492	110	101	121	179	44	180		443	237	225	385	587	192	180	776	608	359	341
Carlisle	301	217	233	192	344	356	273	259	275		222	304	602	151	571	444	333	150	523	341
Chester	185	355	95	73	218	240	147	167	147	138		114	415	373	357	243	555	372	375	137
Derby	123	394	138	39	190	178	121	96	140	189	71		315	436	315	312	637	454	261	251
Dover	73	574	285	184	173	81	195	127	239	374	258	196		726	391	539	935	752	203	538
Edinburgh	378	123	327	286	438	433	367	338	365	94	232	271	451		723	616	233	72	650	489
Exeter	171	566	202	161	82	171	75	218	119	355	222	196	243	449		372	904	721	389	460
Fishguard	262	494	56	176	233	291	156	271	112	276	151	194	335	383	231		777	594	533	272
Fort William	508	158	440	399	551	563	480	466	482	207	345	396	581	145	562	483		183	856	671
Glasgow	394	150	326	285	437	449	366	352	378	93	231	282	467	45	448	369	114		673	488
Harwich	71	527	286	166	176	126	195	66	223	325	233	162	126	404	242	331	532	418		497
Holyhead	261	430	113	153	288	316	211	243	212	212	85	156	334	304	286	169	417	303	309	
Hull	168	348	229	143	255	223	226	124	244	155	132	98	251	225	301	285	362	250	181	217
Inverness	537	105	482	445	594	590	528	497	524	253	387	430	601	159	603	529	66	176	563	463
Leeds	190	322	173	111	261	251	206	148	212	115	78	74	269	199	268	229	322	210	214	163
Leicester	98	417	151	39	166	153	112	68	139	208	94	28	171	294	187	207	415	301	134	183
Lincoln	136	382	186	85	217	191	163	86	190	180	123	51	213	259	238	245	387	273	152	208
Liverpool	205	334	104	94	235	260	164	184	164	116	17	88	278	210	239	160	323	211	250	94
Manchester	192	332	133	81	228	247	167	154	172	115	38	58	265	209	242	189	322	210	220	123
Newcastle	271	230	270	209	348	326	295	231	310	58	175	164	344	107	370	326	257	143	297	260
Norwich	107	487	267	155	212	162	221	60	237	287	210	139	169	364	277	331	494	380	63	299
Nottingham	123	388	154	50	189	178	132	84	152	185	87	16	196	265	207	210	392	278	150	172
Oxford	56	464	157	62	92	99	66	79	107	256	128	98	129	341	139	207	461	340	134	202
Penzance	282	683	313	268	193	269	186	329	230	466	333	307	354	560	111	342	673	559	353	397
Plymouth	213	614	244	199	124	213	117	260	161	397	264	238	285	491	42	273	604	490	284	328
Preston	216	302	144	105	256	271	185	198	190	85	49	100	289	179	266	200	292	180	264	125
Sheffield	162	358	158	75	227	217	163	124	176	145	78	36	235	235	248	214	352	240	190	163
Southampton	79	530	202	128	32	60	75	136	119	322	194	164	149	416	111	231	520	415	150	283
Stranraer	410	235	342	301	453	465	382	368	384	109	247	298	483	133	464	385	199	85	434	321
Swansea	196	506	76	126	162	220	85	216	41	289	151	165	280	383	160	71	496	382	264	189
Worcester	114	428	98	26	131	168	60	116	75	211	88	65	187	305	135	155	418	304	182	152
York	196	309	197	134	273	251	215	157	242	116	102	89	269	186	290	253	323	211	223	187

MILES

KILOMETRES

	Hull	Inverness	Leeds	Leicester	Lincoln	Liverpool	Manchester	Newcastle	Norwich	Nottingham	Oxford	Penzance	Plymouth	Preston	Sheffield	Southampton	Stranraer	Swansea	Worcester	York
LONDON	270	864	306	158	219	330	309	436	172	198	90	454	343	348	261	127	660	315	183	315
Aberdeen	560	169	518	671	615	538	534	370	784	624	747	1099	988	486	576	853	378	814	689	497
Aberystwyth	369	776	278	243	304	167	214	435	430	248	253	504	393	232	254	325	550	122	148	317
Birmingham	230	716	179	63	137	151	130	336	249	80	100	431	320	169	121	206	484	203	42	216
Bournemouth	410	956	420	267	349	378	367	560	341	304	148	311	200	412	365	51	729	261	211	439
Brighton	359	950	404	246	307	418	398	525	261	286	159	433	343	436	349	97	748	354	270	404
Bristol	364	850	332	180	262	264	269	475	356	212	106	299	188	298	262	121	615	137	97	346
Cambridge	200	800	238	109	138	296	248	372	97	135	127	529	418	319	200	219	592	348	187	253
Cardiff	393	843	341	224	306	264	277	499	381	245	172	370	259	306	283	192	618	66	121	389
Carlisle	249	407	185	335	290	187	185	93	462	298	412	750	639	137	233	518	175	465	340	187
Chester	212	623	126	151	198	27	61	282	338	140	206	536	425	79	126	312	398	243	142	164
Derby	158	692	119	45	82	142	93	264	224	26	158	494	383	161	58	264	480	266	105	143
Dover	404	967	433	275	343	447	426	554	272	315	208	570	459	465	378	240	777	451	301	433
Edinburgh	362	256	320	473	417	338	336	172	586	426	549	901	790	288	378	669	214	616	491	299
Exeter	484	970	431	301	383	385	389	595	446	333	224	179	68	428	399	179	747	257	217	467
Fishguard	459	851	369	333	394	257	304	525	533	338	333	550	439	322	344	372	620	114	429	407
Fort William	583	106	518	668	623	520	518	414	795	631	742	1083	972	470	566	837	320	798	673	520
Glasgow	402	283	338	484	439	340	338	230	612	447	547	900	789	290	386	668	137	615	489	340
Harwich	291	906	344	216	245	402	354	478	101	241	216	568	457	425	306	241	698	429	293	359
Holyhead	349	745	262	295	335	151	198	418	481	277	325	639	528	201	262	455	517	304	245	301
Hull		615	90	145	61	196	151	190	240	148	262	663	552	180	103	412	425	433	272	63
Inverness	382		579	729	673	605	604	428	842	682	816	1159	1049	555	634	925	417	872	747	552
Leeds	56	358		158	108	119	64	148	277	116	272	613	502	90	58	378	360	369	220	39
Leicester	90	453	98		82	187	138	301	187	42	119	480	369	206	105	225	510	282	109	174
Lincoln	38	418	67	51		192	137	245	169	56	201	562	451	185	72	307	465	340	192	124
Liverpool	122	376	74	116	119		55	253	360	167	251	563	452	50	119	357	362	270	169	158
Manchester	94	375	40	86	85	34		212	306	119	230	568	457	48	64	325	360	295	164	103
Newcastle	118	266	92	187	152	157	132		414	254	412	774	663	203	206	518	262	517	378	127
Norwich	149	523	174	116	105	224	190	257		198	224	626	515	354	241	299	637	439	283	293
Nottingham	92	424	72	26	35	104	74	158	123		156	512	401	167	64	262	473	283	122	134
Oxford	163	507	169	74	125	156	143	256	139	97		402	291	272	217	106	587	230	95	291
Penzance	412	720	381	298	349	350	353	481	389	318	250		126	597	560	357	925	436	396	645
Plymouth	343	652	312	229	280	281	284	412	320	249	181	78		486	447	246	814	325	285	534
Preston	112	345	56	128	115	31	30	126	220	104	169	371	302		113	375	312	322	203	126
Sheffield	64	394	36	65	45	74	40	128	150	40	135	348	278	70		323	490	336	163	90
Southampton	256	575	235	140	191	222	202	322	186	163	66	222	153	233	201		679	257	193	398
Stranraer	264	259	224	317	289	225	224	163	396	294	365	575	506	194	254	422		461	515	362
Swansea	269	542	229	175	211	168	183	321	273	176	143	271	202	200	209	160	398		161	418
Worcester	169	464	137	68	119	105	102	235	176	76	59	246	177	126	101	120	320	100		257
York	39	343	24	108	77	98	64	79	182	83	181	401	332	78	56	247	225	260	160	

Year Planner 2022

	S	S	M	T	W	T	F	S	S	M	T	W	T	F	S	S	
January	1	2	3	4	5	6	7	8	9	10	11	12	13	14	15	16	1
February			1	2	3	4	5	6	7	8	9	10	11	12	13	1
March			1	2	3	4	5	6	7	8	9	10	11	12	13	1
April						1	2	3	4	5	6	7	8	9	10	1
May	1	2	3	4	5	6	7	8	9	10	11	12	13	14	15	1
June			1	2	3	4	5	6	7	8	9	10	11	12	1
July						1	2	3	4	5	6	7	8	9	10	1
August		1	2	3	4	5	6	7	8	9	10	11	12	13	14	1
September				1	2	3	4	5	6	7	8	9	10	11	1
October	1	2	3	4	5	6	7	8	9	10	11	12	13	14	15	16	1
November			1	2	3	4	5	6	7	8	9	10	11	12	13	1
December				1	2	3	4	5	6	7	8	9	10	11	1